MANAGING
SERVICE INDUSTRIES

MANAGING SERVICE INDUSTRIES

Organizational Practices in a Postindustrial Economy

PETER K. MILLS

BALLINGER PUBLISHING COMPANY
Cambridge, Massachusetts
A Subsidiary of Harper & Row, Publishers, Inc.

International Standard Book Number: 0-88730-011-1

Library of Congress Catalog Card Number: 85-30678

Printed in the United States of America

Library of Congress Cataloging-in-Publication Data

Mills, Peter K., 1943–
  Managing service industries.

  Bibliography: p.
  Includes index.
  1. Service industries—Management. I. Title.
HD9980.5.M55 1986   658   85-30678
ISBN 0-88730-011-1

CONTENTS

v

LIST OF FIGURES

LIST OF TABLES

PREFACE

The shift to postindustrialism, or a service economy, is an uneasy transition. The discomfort stems from the fact that although three out of every four workers are engaged in service jobs, service organizations have manifested slower productivity growth than their manufacturing counterparts.

This book focuses on the organization and governance of people in services. Its topics are selective and not exhaustive. The book is primarily intended for advanced students in management seeking an understanding of some fundamental principles of how service organizations function.

I would like to thank Professors John Skår and Bo Sellstedt of the University of Stockholm, Sweden, for stimulating my interest in service sector organizations. I am also indebted to many who have contributed to the preparation of the manuscript. Special thanks to Martha Carpenter for her encouragement and suggestions. Appreciation is extended also to Maria De Benedetti, Lowell Dwyer, Melinda Hall, Karen Kress, Ronald March, and Steve Robbins for their comments. Several people assisted with the typing including Candy Goins, Lillian Cifelli, and Liz Caravelli. Finally, much thanks to the editors for their patience and many penetrating comments.

1 POSTINDUSTRIAL ORGANIZATIONS

The Industrial Revolution emerged in Western Europe around the middle of the 1700s and reached its zenith in the United States with the dawning of the twentieth century. By then, the United States and most of Western Europe had become strongly industrial societies. Fueling their economies were work organizations, in particular industrial or manufacturing organizations—coalitions of sometimes diverse interest groups or individuals cooperating in order to accomplish some common outcome or output.

Over the past three decades, a pronounced structural transition has been changing the work world of industrial societies. This second Industrial Revolution is characterized by the transformation of previously recognized industrial societies into service-oriented societies, and it is in every sense as dynamic as the industrial experience.

Since the turn of this century, the service sector of the economy in most developed societies has shown remarkable growth (see Table 1-1). The advent of postindustrialism dramatically indicates that today more of the employable labor force is engaged in service-type organizations than in manufacturing organizations. The service sector encompasses the major areas of trade (retail and wholesale), finance, insurance, communications, public utilities, transportation, government, health care, education, business (accountants, consultants), and personal services.

1

Table 1-1.   Employment Breakdown in EEC Countries from 1963 to 1978 (*percent of total*).

Country	Sector	Year 1963	1968	1973	1978
Belgium	Agriculture	4%	3%	2%	1%
	Manufacture	51	48	45	40
	Service	45	49	53	59
Denmark	Agriculture	7	—	3	3
	Manufacture	43	—	37	32
	Service	50	—	60	65
France	Agriculture	8	6	4	3
	Manufacture	47	45	45	41
	Service	45	49	51	56
Germany	Agriculture	4	3	3	3
	Manufacture	55	54	51	48
	Service	41	43	46	49
Ireland	Agriculture	11	8	6	5
	Manufacture	36	39	40	38
	Service	53	53	54	57
Italy	Agriculture	14	11	9	8
	Manufacture	53	53	52	46
	Service	33	36	38	46
Netherlands	Agriculture	5	3	2	2
	Manufacture	45	43	40	35
	Service	50	54	58	63
UK	Agriculture	6	4	4	3
	Manufacture	45	45	42	39
	Service	48	51	54	58

Source: Calculated from data presented by Gershuny and Miles (1983). (These data are approximations.)

Table 1-2 indicates the distribution of employment by sector in the United States since 1900. The table shows a steady, pronounced growth in the service sector and a concomitant decrease in the percentage of people engaged in manufacturing and agriculture organizations.

Postindustrialism is the age of information. If the industrial revolution can be characterized as the substitution of machines for man-

Table 1-2. Distribution of Labor Force (%) for the United States (*1900 to 1980*).

Year	Sector		
	Agriculture	Manufacture	Service
1900	42%	28%	30%
1910	35	31	34
1920	29	33	38
1930	26	30	44
1940	22	32	46
1950	13	36	51
1960	7	35	58
1970	3	32	65
1980	3	27	70

Source: Statistical Abstract of the United States (1985), U.S. Department of Commerce, Department of the Census; Historical Statistics of the United States: Colonial Times to 1970, U.S. Department of Commerce, Department of the Census.

power as a more productive source of energy, then postindustrialism is characterized by the substitution of new information processing techniques for many roles previously performed by people.

THE PATH OF THE LABOR TRANSITION

Although it is widely recognized that as a society advances economically there is labor movement from one sector to another (Clark 1957), it is of interest to note just how the labor change to the service-sector organizations has occurred. At first glance it appears that the rapid growth of service organizations is emerging from the reduction of the labor force in the agricultural sector. For example, in the United States in the year 1900, as much as 42 percent of the labor force was involved in agricultural activities, but only 3 percent by 1980. Over the same period, service sector employment rose from 30 percent to 70 percent (see Table 1-2). But the full picture is not so simple.

A definitive explanation for the mobility of labor across sectors has not been forthcoming, but two approaches seem reasonable. One explanation centers around a sequential labor flow. This hypothesis suggests that the development of industrialization created a tremen-

Figure 1-1. The Movement of Civilian Labor into Services.

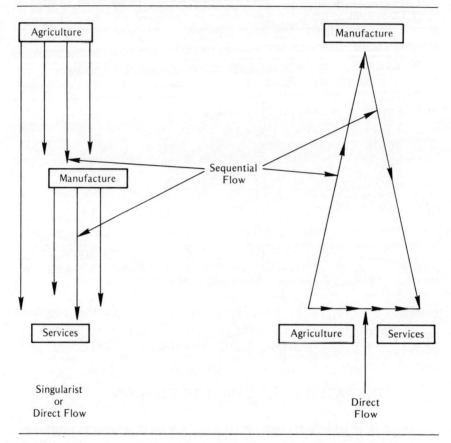

dous demand for human labor as people were needed to tend the newly created machines (see Figure 1-1). Around the same period, the primary or agricultural sector had begun to improve the efficiency of its operations. Farmers discovered that by substituting machines for human labor they could dramatically improve the productivity of their farms. This resulted in excess human labor in agriculture and a migration of such redundant labor force from the rural areas to the urban areas where industrial and manufacturing organizations were springing up. The migration was also facilitated by the higher wage rates that were offered by manufacturing organizations. Consequently, a mutually beneficial relationship developed between the emerging industrial sector and the agricultural sector as the demand for labor by manufacturing organizations absorbed much of the newly redundant farm labor. Thus, the labor force shifted from the farms to the cities. Between 1870 and 1920 both the manufacturing and service sectors were expanding. However, the manufacturing sector showed a more pronounced growth pattern (Fuchs 1981). Victor Fuchs further suggests that the movement of labor employment from manufacturing to services was due to the rapid rate of productivity growth of the manufacturing sector because of increasing technological efficiency (Fuchs 1968, 1969). And replaying the story of the agricultural sector, a labor redundancy emerged that gravitated to the developing service sector.

A second explanation of the labor mobility may be thought of as the direct or singularist labor flow (see Figure 1-1). This pattern appears to characterize the contemporary movement of human labor from agriculture and manufacturing sectors to the service sector. Table 1-1 shows that over the last thirty years the service sector has expanded first by a decrease of the agricultural sector and more recently by decreases in both manufacturing and agriculture. The fundamental premise of the singularist proposition is that the service and service-line activities have been complementary and essential to the production and distribution of mass produced goods for both the agriculture and manufacturing sectors.

DISTINGUISHING FEATURES OF SERVICE ORGANIZATIONS

There is no overwhelming consensus among social scientists as to a clear distinction between service and manufacturing organizations. A major reason for this is the difficulty in defining just what is a service. We will adopt Leonard Berry's definition that "a good is an object, a device, a thing: a service is a deed, a performance, an effort. Although the performance of most services is supported by tangibles, the essence of what is bought is performance rendered by one party for another" (1984). Two contemporary criteria are most often used to distinguish services from manufacturing organizations. The first is that the output of services is intangible; the second is the closeness of the consumer to the producer (Fuchs 1968).

The output of services is abstract and cannot be reasonably stored, a situation in clear contrast to that of the tangible objects produced by manufacturing organizations. The abstractness in output is a critical demarcation because it suggests that there can be no accumulation of inventory. Products from a manufacturing organization are generally produced at one point in time and consumed at some later point. In some instances, the time gap between production and consumption can be quite long (Sasser 1976). In services the consumption of the output is immediate. One would have difficulty conceiving of how to hold a space on a train or an airplane (Miller and Rice 1967). If the service is not consumed or used immediately, it is forever lost, and the waste of the service inevitably repeats itself. Inaccurately, we tend to conceive of the service as waiting to be consumed. A more precise view would be that the service is being wasted. Such services that fail to be utilized invariably add to the overall cost of production. This is certainly the situation in the advertising industry, where it is often extremely difficult to direct the service solely at the potential market segment. Further, the perishable or short-lived nature of services tends to create a vulnerable situation for the organization by reducing the buffer of inventories that is usually vital in the effectiveness of a manufacturing organization.

The second characteristic of service organizations, which emerges from the first, is the closeness of the consumer of the service to the producer of the service (Fuchs 1968). There is direct personal contact in the production of most services, suggesting that the provider of the service (the employee) and the consumer must interact in order for the delivery of the service to be complete. The employee's role in this kind of interface is highly significant. To miss this pivotal role of the service employee is to fail to capture the essence of service organizations, for the service employees dispensing the output directly to the consumer, as Sasser (1976) observes, are actually mini-factories unto themselves. The activities of these individuals transcend mere production of the service. The employees are, in a very real sense, both producing and selling the service to the consumer concurrently.

But the personal interface between the employee and the consumer also suggests that the consumer (client/consumer) is actively involved in what J. D. Thompson (1962) refers to as a transaction with the employee in which information is exchanged. Information is the fundamental raw material of service organizations. It is what the service provider works on in order to generate the service. Much of this information is secured directly from clients/customers. For example, insurance agents must secure information from potential clients in order to provide the best policy; financial planners must obtain information from clients about income, family makeup, age, style of living, and expectations in order to provide sound financial services. Thus, the idea of organizations as information-processing entities (Galbraith 1973) is very descriptive of service organizations.

Our discussion on attempting to isolate the unique features of services and manufacturing organizations has been restricted to ideal types. But in reality, it is difficult to segment the service sector from the manufacturing sector within organizations where both activities concurrently exist. In this peculiar symbiotic relationship in which the service functions are intricately intertwined with the manufacturing activities, problems arise in attempting to isolate the output of the two functions. To some extent, such problems can be resolved by a slight change in our perspective of the activities involved. Usually, these service activities are to be found in areas often referred to as the support areas—for example, legal services, personnel training, industrial relations, marketing activities, technocratic staff—that involve the maintenance of predominantly technical equipment and other activities in the organization's administration. It is highly likely that these activities could be physically removed to separate domains. Indeed, the removal of such producer services (R&D, data processing, purchasing) and of distribution services such as advertising and marketing is partially responsible for the rapid growth of the service sector (Stanback et al. 1981). The contracting out of such services is an attempt to lower the cost of production, as these types of services can be produced more cheaply by outside contractors.

Far more problematic is the rather general nature of the characteristics we are forced to adopt as attributes of a service organization. This is unavoidably so because services are by their very nature complex and ambiguous organizations. For instance, it was earlier noted that service organizations produce an intangible output and manufacturing organizations, a tangible output. But Fuchs (1968) raises some interesting questions regarding this characteristic. If a college professor lectures to his or her students, few would disagree that a service is being rendered. If, on the other hand, the professor writes a book, his action gives rise to the question of whether he is performing a manufacturing or a service activity. The book in all economic senses is tangible, which is not a primary characteristic of services output. It is often very difficult to clarify such multi-dimensional output effectively.

INTERDEPENDENT ATTRIBUTES

It is of interest to note some features that emerge from the interdependence between manufacturing and service firms where the attributes of one sector may affect those of another. With the decline of the manufacturing sector and the concurrent expansion of the service sector, there are some transferable effects from the former to the latter.

Manufacture	*Service*
1. Rational planning	1. Excess capacity
2. Elimination of unproductive factors	2. Uncertain environment (new differential demand)
3. Efficiency gains exported to the service sector	3. Creating an awareness-attention-drawing organization

Generally, manufacturing organizations have the ability to rationalize or schedule the production process, which serves to eliminate excess capacity. The problems with measuring service output make it difficult to rationalize the production function. Thus, services tend to entertain excess capacity, and this affects productivity. Further, manufacturing organizations lend themselves more readily to innovations in the production function that will tend to reduce the labor force. The labor efficiency gains experienced by the manufacturing sector organizations can be transferred to services in the form of excess labor. Service organizations do not lend themselves, generally, to such production gains, and they tend to be disproportionately labor intensive.

THE SIZE DIMENSION

One of the germane features of services, and one that is usually most visible, is the tendency of these organizations to be small. In the United States, over 60 percent of all service workers are employed in organizations with fewer than 100 employees, whereas 70 percent of

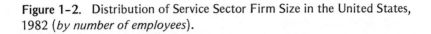

Figure 1-2. Distribution of Service Sector Firm Size in the United States, 1982 (*by number of employees*).

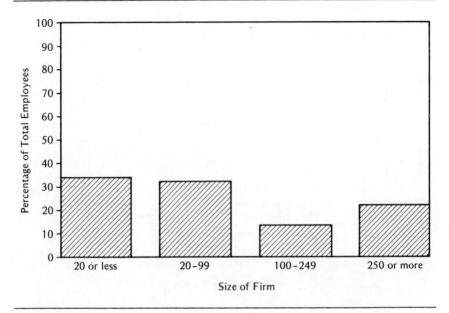

Source: Statistical Abstract of the United States (1985), U.S. Department of Commerce, Department of the Census.

all workers in manufacturing are in organizations of 100 employees or more (see Figures 1-2 and 1-3). This phenomenon does not appear to be unique to the United States but is pervasive throughout the developed economies. For example, in Sweden, in 1975, 46 percent of all manufacturing employees were in organizations with more than 500 employees and 80 percent of service employees were in organizations with less than 500 employees (National Bureau of Statistics, Sweden, 1975).

This is not to suggest that there are no large service organizations to rival in size their manufacturing counterparts. Bank of America Corporation has 91,000 employees, Citicorp has 64,000 both domestic and international, and Sears employs 450,000 people (*Moody's Bank and Finance Manual*, Vol. 1, 1984; *Moody's Industrial Manual*, Vol. 2, 1984). Currently, however, such large service organizations are not widespread and appear to be exceptions rather than the rule.

A paramount reason for the tendency of services to be relatively small in size is the nature of service output. As mentioned above, ser-

Figure 1-3. Distribution of Manufacturing Firm Size in the United States, 1982 (*by number of employees*).

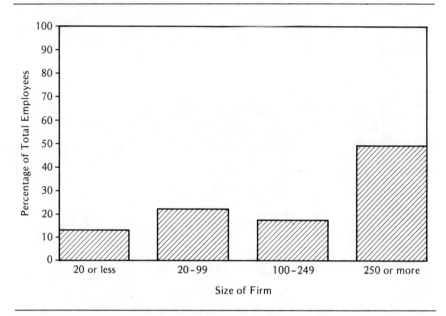

Size of Firm

Source: Statistical Abstract of the United States (1985), U.S. Department of Commerce, Department of the Census.

vice outputs are generally intangible, so they cannot be easily stored and must be delivered to the customer. This restricts or limits the market of any individual establishment. In other words, the personal delivery system in the service firm's production function makes it more efficient to administer the output in small units (Stanback et al. 1981).

The small size of services may also be due to the capital structure and competitiveness of these firms. Most service organizations require relatively little capital investment to begin since what is being transferred to the consumer is primarily information in the form of effort or performance by the service provider. This makes the ease of entry into the service sector a relatively simple process and creates a dynamic environment with more competitive market segments, as opposed to the general oligopolistic nature of manufacturing industries. In addition, the competition in services is intense primarily because the innovations in these organizations are so easily transferable and can be readily adopted by competitors. Small organizations are more adaptive to dynamic environments than large firms. Because they are less able to manage their environments, service organizations have been forced to develop mechanisms that allow them to more readily respond to change.

PUBLIC AND PRIVATE SECTOR DIMENSIONS

Traditionally, organization theorists and other social scientists have ignored public sector organizations. But it seems quite clear in studying service organizations and developing generic models, some attention should be directed to the public arena, that is, public administration, education and research, medical care, social security, public safety, and so on. Although the private sector service organizations constitute the largest segment of services, the proportion of public services is not insignificant. Approximately one out of every six workers in the total labor force is employed by public sector organizations.

Fundamental differences appear to exist between these public and private sector service organizations. One distinction between the sectors, as Warwick (1975) argues, is that of organization origin. Private sector firms generally come into existence under entrepreneurial conditions, whereas public sector organizations are always created by some higher controlling body. Another area of significant divergence is in the output objective within their respective environments. The primary objective of the private service organization is to extract resources from its environment, that is, to make a profit within market mechanisms. Traditionally, this has been the primary criterion on which its performance has been based. Private services exist to provide services to the market at some optimum price. On the other hand, the public service organizations—for example, welfare agencies, law enforcement, fire protection, public transportation—have essentially the reverse objective, that is, to return resources to their environment. The service output generated by the public service organization is intended to be provided to the buyer or consumer at some minimum price. The cheaper the services rendered to the community, the greater performance the public organization is thought to display; hence the notion of these organizations being nonprofit.

Although public service organizations often use acquisition of resources as a measure of effectiveness, such resources are nevertheless intended to achieve output goals.

CONCERNS FOR THE GROWTH OF SERVICES

One of the major concerns of contemporary managers is the issue of productivity. Between the end of World War II and the year 1970, productivity growth within the United States averaged close to 3.2 percent annually. Although the rise was uneven, there has been a pronounced and persistent downward shift in the growth pattern over the latter part of this period that carried over into the decade of the 1970s, as evidenced by the annual average growth rate of 1.5 percent during the years between 1970 and 1980. There is strong concern that a continuing shift of labor resources to the service sector has not generated a corresponding rise in their contribution to the gross national product.

Several studies suggest that the productivity in service organizations has grown less rapidly than in agriculture and manufacturing sectors (Fuchs 1968; Grossman and Fuchs 1975; Kavis et al. 1978). It would appear that the rise of postindustrial organizations has been accompanied by a lag in output per worker relative to the performance of workers in manufacturing organizations.

One obvious problem that arises when comparing the productivity between the manufacturing and service sectors is that changes in input for service organizations appear to be the only available indicator of output change, making it extremely difficult to determine productivity growth, if any, for service firms (Ward 1973). A notable exception has been the retail service trades, where it has been possible to isolate output in terms of volume of sales. Studies undertaken in both Sweden and England found a marked difference in productivity among the service organizations within the retail industries and in some cases a higher productivity level than in manufacturing industries (Skår 1971; Ward 1973). However, the retail industry is subject to some unique peculiarities not found in most other areas of the service sector. The retail trades tend to be made up of large organizations that operate in monopolistic states, and these organizations are receptive to technological innovations. These factors coupled with the usually fixed labor costs in this sector distort the downward productivity picture prevalent in most services (Kaldor 1966).

The general opinion seems to be that factors in services such as less intensive use of advanced technology, relatively weak unions, quality of labor, trade-offs in manufacturing of capital for labor that increase productivity, and problems in the accuracy of the tools employed in the measurement of services do play a part in the productivity disparity among the economic sectors. However, it appears that the postindustrial development is an uncomfortable social transition that may pose several interesting economic consequences. This is because the productivity of labor is of fundamental concern to society.

A detrimental effect of the expansion of services could be a lower aggregate economic productivity, both in quality and quantity of output. This assumption is based on the labor intensiveness of services and the vital role the employees are thought to play in the production function of service organizations. The assumption here is that labor-intensive organizations generally experience relatively lower productivity gains than do capital-intensive organizations. Of the four elementary factors of production—capital, material, energy, and labor—labor has traditionally been recognized as the most costly for the manager. Consequently, management has traditionally moved toward the mechanization and job rationalization of their organizations whenever possible with usually favorable economic results, especially within manufacturing organizations.

If there is indeed a productivity lag in postindustrial organizations and it continues unheeded, then a likely future consequence will be a tendency to retard aggregate economic productivity gains and therefore efforts within the social system to maintain price stability. The U.S. economy has to expand by at least 3 to 4 percent per annum in order to absorb the people entering the labor force for the first time (high school graduates, college graduates, housewives). With the development of postindustrial organizations, this vital growth objective would seem to be threatened. Gershuny and Miles (1983) have shown that the persistent increase in employment is due primarily to the relatively low productivity of service sector organizations.

There is an association between expansion of the services and price stability in postindustrial economies. The necessity for economic growth seems inevitably to foster the proliferation of service organizations as the manufacturing sector organizations become more efficient and as pressure is exerted by an expanding labor force. But the service sector organizations do not seem to respond readily to efficient mass production techniques. Thus, over time there will be an inevitable increase in price levels. Indeed, Fitzsimons and Sullivan (1982) have noted that over the past decade, services have shown a faster rate of price increases than goods. This finding is consistent with Heilbroner's (1980) observation that the inflation spiral, pervasive and persistent during the 1970s, may have been partially attributed to the growth of low-producing service organizations.

The expansion of service may affect prices in another way. Service organizations compete with manufacturing and agriculture organizations for the consumer's disposable income. When any economic sector competes with other sectors for a share of the disposable income, its effectiveness is primarily due to the prices it charges for its output. Thus, if the service sector industry is to be generally profitable, it is faced with either increasing the productivity of the labor force or increasing prices for its output. When there is an increase in labor productivity, profitability can be realized, relative to one's competitors, by keeping prices the same or lowering them. If, however, the productivity of workers in the service sector is decreasing, as appears to be the case, the prices of the output will have to increase. In essence, the decrease in service productivity over a given period will inflate prices of services if a given profit level is to be realized. This inflationary spiral will decrease real per capita growth and could eventually affect the living standards of postindustrial societies.

ANTIQUATED ATTITUDES ABOUT SERVICES

As service managers grope for methods to deal with their organizations' problems, it becomes strikingly clear that there is a conspicuous lack of information directly relevant to the operation of their firms. This information shortage would seem to reflect a lack of understanding of services by society in general. One paramount source of the public's negative attitude toward services is tradition (Galbraith 1969). Early economists strongly questioned the value of services to the social system. Adam Smith, perhaps reflecting the consensus among his contemporaries, regarded service organizations as generally parasitic in the economic arena and viewed the productive contribution of these organizations to society with some skepticism. Smith was of the myopic opinion that service organizations were being maintained at the expense of the agricultural and manufacturing economic subsectors (Smith 1904).

The eminent economist Thorstein Veblen (1904) was emphatic in his outright dismissal of services, which he viewed as unimportant to the economic well-being of society. Veblen failed to consider services as separate or distinct entities within the larger economic system. He purported with ample justification and lucidity that a theory of modern economies is primarily a theory of the "machine process" in reference to manufacturing organizations, with services playing a miniscule role. Veblen further asserted that "brute" service organizations contribute nothing substantial to output and therefore serve as an excessive burden on the income of others directly involved in industries and eventually serve merely to undermine the vitality of the community. This erstwhile view toward the services is not at odds with views held by some contemporary theorists. Reubens (1981), for example, suggests that the employment in services is an unproductive use of economic resources and that the service sector is partially responsible for many economic problems in the United States. Although services have indeed developed and taken on new meaning in contemporary society, they have not lost the traditional ambiguity of being both an economic necessity and a social strain. It still is feared that expansion of the service sector could have a stifling effect on the manufacturing sector.

MACRO-ORGANIZATIONAL PROBLEMS OF THE POSTINDUSTRIAL ORGANIZATIONS

It was earlier noted that one of the major problems facing service organizations concerns productivity. As a result there is pressure on managers of these organizations for productivity improvement. This pressure often forces managers to take radical steps within their organizations. Faced with a dearth of information directly pertinent to the operations of their organizations, many managers have adopted macro-organization concepts that have proven effective in manufacturing organizations. This action has led some scholars to proclaim that, many of the imported techniques are counterproductive because they are being adopted with too little reflection. It makes as much sense, they say, to use manufacturing theories in services as it does to use agricultural concepts in manufacturing organizations (Davis and Taylor 1972; Davis 1984). Take, for example, the theories regarding the structuring of organizations, the internal arrangement of the organization's task activities or the roles of individuals. Within an industrial or manufacturing organization there is empirical evidence to suggest that structure is significantly influenced by the type of technology employed therein (Woodward 1965; Zwerman 1970). In order to optimize production, it is of the utmost importance to organize people around the task activities being used to produce the firm's output. This would seem intuitively sensible since the tangible nature of a manufacturing organization's input and the subsequent concrete output make it possible to manipulate its production process into predictable activities. There is also a buffering of core technologies from environmental influences within these organizations, which serves to rationalize job activities.

But clearly, service organizations depend more directly on their external environment, are smaller in size, and require more diverse measures of organization effectiveness than do manufacturing organizations. Is it therefore just as sensible to adopt similar task and job rationalization assumptions about service organizations given the pronounced differences between sectors? The adoption of such strategies may indeed be counterproductive exercises from a macro-organization perspective.

THE PURPOSE AND ORGANIZATION
OF THIS BOOK

The intention of this book, as earlier mentioned, is to increase the reader's awareness of how service organizations govern their resources. The aim is to provide a set of principles or laws that are fundamentally pertinent to services in general. In order to do so, the book will draw on contemporary knowledge of service sector organizations and, because relatively little work has been done in this area, generate new models to fill in gaps in this expanding service area.

The analysis will focus on macro-organization issues, specifically on the governance or control of resources within these organizations. If service organizations are to remain viable, managers must come to grips with the cost of organizing or structuring their activities. Improved labor productivity can be realized by considering these costs.

The following chapter examines the external environment of service organizations and the movement of clients/customers across service boundaries into the internal environment of services. It discusses the nature of contracts established between the service provider and clients/customers and presents a typology of service organizations based on the kinds of contracts and the dependency clients/customers have on the service organization.

Chapter 3 discusses the technology of service operations. It examines the types of technologies appropriate for different service encounters. Further, the notion of technology is expanded to include activities of clients/customers in service operations and the techniques involved in the monitoring of production activities.

In Chapter 4 the nature of service organization structure and the essentials of organizing costs are examined. This chapter looks at the factors that affect the designs organizations adopt, using empirical data to compare the dimensions of service organizations with those of manufacturing firms.

The focus of Chapter 5 is the subjective side of structure. It explores the qualitative framework of organizations that guides the service provider's behavior and provides data for the discussion between subjective structures and other service organization properties.

Power is the subject of Chapter 6. Here, the service organization is viewed as an internal market where resources are exchanged and accumulated. The pricing or valuation of resources necessary for providing the service outcome is discussed as an important precursor to the accumulation of resources.

Chapter 7 is concerned with the control of performance within the primary operating core of service organizations. This chapter examines the notions of employee self-control and control loss. Control is also expanded to include the behavior of clients/customers in service operations. Professional distance is discussed as a method of controlling the behavior of clients/customers who are actively involved in service operations.

Chapter 8 deals with the issues of service quality, discussing factors such as moral hazard and adverse selection. Ways to improve the quality of services delivered to clients/customers are also explored.

Chapter 9 examines the socialization of clients/customers as partial employees of service organizations. This chapter looks at the roles of clients/customers in the production of service outputs and examines techniques used to introduce clients/customers to productive behaviors.

Chapter 10 explores the expanding area of professional firms and how they are organized. An in-depth analysis, based on empirical data, of the flexiform structure is presented as a model for optimizing the resources of professional organizations.

The final chapter discusses some problems that will confront future service managers in governing the resources within their organizations. This chapter also summarizes the governance of resources within such organizations.

2 AN ENVIRONMENTAL TAXONOMY

All service organizations exist in external environments—the total set of elements outside of the organization—that have a direct and indirect impact on their performance. The environment of organizations can be divided into two fundamental categories of (1) market or microenvironment, consisting of such factors as consumers, competitors, technological changes, suppliers, and so on and (2) non-market or macroenvironment, including such factors as political activities, government regulations, social and cultural factors, national economic and fiscal policy, demographics, and so on. Generally, organizations are most influenced by their microenvironmental factors because those factors directly affect the strategy and internal workings of the firm.

In order to remain viable, organizations must adapt and display a potential for adaptability to their environments. But such adaptability is based on internal decisions as organizations seek to control their environments by deliberately adjusting to them (Pfeffer 1978). Such adjustment may take the form of the organization selecting its environment, creating new environments, establishing monopolies and oligopolies in order to reduce instability, or using political activity to gain competitive advantages. In sum, organizations select strategies that satisfy the demands of their members or stakeholders.

There is a crucial relationship between service organizations and their environments that is best described as reciprocal interdependence. This means that the external environment is a source of crucial resources on which organizations attempt to draw. Such resources are inputs and are incorporated into the organization in the form of employees, capital, new innovations, clients and customers, raw material, and so on. Simply stated, an organization incorporates input materials from its environment that are then transformed into service output in accordance with the organization's own characteristics and capabilities. The transformed goods or services are then exported back into the environment (Emery and Trist 1965).

In order to stabilize the organization's relationship with the environment service managers must contend with at least two important issues: predicting the major changes occurring in their external environments and determining what impact those changes will have on the operations of their organizations. Of all the environmental factors with which service organizations must deal, the market factors, particularly competitors, are the most crucial for their well-being. Service organizations have to be acutely conscious of competitors for several reasons. First, there is easy transference of innovation from one organization to others. It is very difficult to protect innovation by patents that generate interdependence and interrelatedness. Second, service organizations tend to be relatively small, which makes them vulnerable, small organizations being more likely to fail than larger ones. Their competitiveness is thus increased. Third, the relative ease of entry into service markets increases competition. These factors foster complex competitive environments that generate much market uncertainty or instability. As a result, the competitive bases of the environment must be monitored continually for such unique advantages as price, quality, and responsiveness so that the organization can maintain equilibrium and can survive. Although such monitoring activities are clearly important for the service firm's stability, they are problematic for the service manager because the inability to buffer with inventories on the output side of service organizations decreases the effectiveness of forecasting.

THE MARKET NICHE

One way of coping with these issues is by narrowing the scope of the organizational market environment. By this we mean that the service organization finds a niche within the external market environment that is compatible with the organization's unique characteristics with respect to the services being offered and the markets or clients/customers being served. Large service organizations need to give each store, branch office, and so on enough autonomy to adapt to its unique market environment. What works in Boston may not work in San Francisco.

The selection of a market niche is of immense importance as a preliminary step in adjusting to the environment. By operating in a niche, the organization essentially reduces the number of elements it has to cope with and thus increases its probability of survival. But even such an external sequence can be especially problematical for the service organization because of the uncertainty surrounding crucial information from the market. Environmental uncertainty implies several things to an organization, one of which is that crucial information is difficult to obtain. Another implication is that there is a lack of clarity in the information obtained from the environment (Lawrence and Lorsch 1967) such that the information lends itself to various interpretations. Consequently, it is difficult to ascertain the effects of specific decisions in terms of cost to the organization if the decision is incorrect (Duncan 1972). The decisionmakers in service organizations must therefore operate in a speculative environment that dictates more entrepreneurial risk-taking relative to his/her manufacturing counterparts.

THE ENCOUNTER WITH CLIENTS/CUSTOMERS

Clients and customers are crucial market environmental elements brought into the service operations through service encounters. Although clients and customers are vital to the operations of services, they are simultaneously problematic because their behavior cannot be predicted with any degree of regularity (Bauer 1968), especially in competitive markets. All customers entering the service operation have different demands and expectations. Service employees in direct contact with clients and customers must be environmental boundary spanners attempting to reduce uncertainty by performing adaptation activities as representatives of organizations (Bowen and Schneider, 1985).

The nature of the encounter between the service employee and customer reflects the nature of the environmental niche in which the service organization exists. It is largely through the encounter that service organizations extract resources from the external environment and in turn transmit their output back to the environment. Thus, the encounter provides some insight as to the kind of environmental uncertainty or complexity the organization faces.

To a significant degree service encounters emerge as social interactions in which clients/customers, as important environmental elements, are brought into the service operations by directly transacting with service employees (Thompson 1962; McCallum and Harrison 1985). This means that in every contact episode, or each time the service employee interacts with clients/customers, there is a direct exchange with the environment. However, it is more accurate to view the service organization's direct link to its environment as a socioeconomic situation. In each encounter, clients/customers are physically in the presence of the service employee (Goffman 1983), and the encounter forms the fundamental framework through which resources are exchanged between the service organization and its environment.

More specifically, the encounter is an economic transaction in which the organization, through its employee, makes a sacrifice or gives up resources in the form of effort, skill, information, and so on in exchange for some gain from the client/customer in terms of money, cooperation, and other resources. Such exchanges are tacit bargaining processes in which the service firm's direct relationship with its environment, specifically its clients/customers, is broadened as the output of one participant becomes the input of another. Thus the service encounters are, for all practical purposes, production processes. The economic or production nature of the service firm's direct encounter with its environment underscores Sasser's (1976) observation of this exchange being a "mini-factory" within the service organization. Each time the service organization makes contact with clients/customers within its environment an attempt is being made to obtain valuable resources while simultaneously relinquishing others in exchange. What makes these environmental encounters productive is that they must yield a surplus in excess of what existed before. Thus, the nature of the market environment will determine the kind of interaction the service organization will have with clients/customers and the resources exchanged.

ENCOUNTERS AS SERVICE CONTRACTS

The encounter between the service organization and its clients/customers is best viewed as a contract. Within this contract, clients/customers engage the service organization to perform some service on their behalf. The contract also entails the client/customer delegating some authority or decisionmaking right to the service provider (Jensen and Meckling 1976). For example, clients contract with their stockbroker to invest their money, and the broker is given the authority to make decisions that would optimize such investments; patrons in restaurants contract with the establishment for a meal and give the restaurant the authority to make decisions that would make such meals satisfying; patients in health care contract with the physician and delegate some decisionmaking authority to the physician in providing the appropriate care and agree to adhere to the doctor's instructions and requests.

A set of mutual expectations involving a pattern of rights, privileges, and obligations is either implicit or explicit in the contract. The contract sets forth the "internal rules of the game." This is crucial not only because it establishes some degree of specificity as to the rights of the client/customer and the service provider, but more importantly, because it establishes the performance criteria on which the parties are evaluated and the kinds of payoffs they can expect (Fama and Jensen 1983).

Service contracts reduce the uncertainty of one important element in the external environment, namely clients and customers. Contracts obligate the participants to certain patterns of behavioral expectations and thus increase the ability to correctly predict and forecast future events. Thus, contracts between a service organization and clients/customers are a useful mechanism for the organization in optimizing the allocation of resources and adjusting to environmental contingencies.

ENCOUNTER COSTS AND OBLIGATIONS

The encounter between the service organization and the client/customer is not without some cost. Encounters, as contracts, are established for the exchange of resources. In order for the parties to undertake the exchange of resources it is necessary that they seek each other out, which generates costs in terms of time and energy. If the client/customer and the service provider are to succeed in establishing a meaningful and equitable contract, it is in the best interest of both to inform one another of the kinds of resources and opportunities that may exist. The conveying of such information will require resources.

Further, both the service provider and the client/customer may not always act in the best interest of one another. For example, the stockbroker may engage in speculative investment with the client's money; the physician may perform an incompetent or ill-conceived diagnosis of the patient; lawyers may devote little time to the client's problems; restaurants may reduce the portions of certain foods served to the patrons. Conversely, consumers may return items that have been misused; customers/clients may not pay their bills, and so on. In order to reduce the potential for such activities, cost will be incurred in policing and monitoring the behavior of both the service provider and clients/customers to ensure that they meet their contractual obligations.

Generally, the encounters between service organizations and clients/customers entail some fundamental obligations or understanding. One understanding is that in all encounters there is a basic expectation that the same or equal service will be dispensed to all consumers, no consumer being favored or disfavored over others. Another understanding is that clients/customers will be treated with courtesy—that the service provider will give immediate attention to the client's/customer's request and perform such request with words, gestures, and manner that indicate or signal approval of the client/customer and some pleasure at having the consumer in the encounter (Goffman 1983). These two principles, equality and courtesy, are fundamental expectations in service encounters and imply a minimum standard expected of service organizations in the exchange of resources with clients/customers.

At the core of all encounters is the notion of equity, or mutual agreement or understanding that the resources being exchanged in the encounter are fair to the participants. The idea of equity involves an input–output ratio and implies that in the exchange of resources in service transactions, clients/customers will compare the service they are receiving with the service being given to others relative to the cost of the service to them. Thus, consumers invariably compare the worth of their services or resources received with those of others by the way they are treated throughout the encounter. Similarly, service providers compare the effort or resources they require to secure client compliance with efforts required of other service providers.

Thus, before mutual agreement can be established in service encounters, the participants to such contracts have to develop standards of comparison (Adams 1965). The exchange that takes place in the transaction is equitable when there is mutual agreement that what the participants possess is of equal value. If inequity is observed, the client/customer may hire an agent with a more favorable input-output ratio to represent him or her (e.g., a teenager may have a parent negotiate an insurance purchase). The same is common with the service provider (e.g., doctors bring in specialists).

Service encounters between the service organization and clients/customers may vary in the quality of the exchange of resources from weak or low encounters to strong or high encounters. High-service encounters entail the exchange of resources that are characterized by a high exchange value (Graen 1976). By this we mean that the education, intelligence, skills, age, health, information, and abilities for the completion of the transaction are costly to secure and therefore scarce. Consumers are relatively more dependent on the service provider when the problems or requests of consumers are complex. Partially responsible for the complexity is the often equivocal nature of the issues being brought to the encounter, which implies that the service provider will be required to secure and process copious amounts of information in order to address complex issues, and much of this information will be equivocal. Since it takes equivocality to reduce equivocality (Weick 1969), the exchange of resources in these encounters is relatively extensive and potentially costly. Health care organizations and educational institutions require resources and skills that are complex and costly to obtain.

Conversely, in low encounters, the resources exchanged in the transaction between the service organization and the client/customer are low in value (Graen 1976). The problems or issues that are brought to the transaction by the consumer are fairly simple. There is a limited exchange of resources because the consumer's problems are unequivocal and activities can be systematized. Consequently, the consumer will have little dependence on the service provider for rendering the service. For example, retail stores, fast food operations, and banks address problems from their customers that are relatively simple and predictable. Such low encounters require resources that are not difficult to secure and thus are low in value.

A TAXONOMY OF SERVICE ORGANIZATIONS

There is a direct association between the kinds of encounters the service organization establishes with clients/customers and the degree of environmental uncertainty involved. Environmental uncertainty is reflected specifically in the complexity of the information exchanged. Consequently, within encounters the service organization's resources that are capable of neutralizing uncertainty become valuable and accordingly more indispensable. Furthermore, the resources, assets, or skills possessed by service organizations are valued not only by the extent to which they can deal with specific market environmental problems that are brought to the organization by client/customers but also by the degree to which their effects can be readily assessed (Williamson 1981).

Two fundamental dimensions can be observed in the interaction between a service organization and its client/customer environment: the nature of the encounter with clients and customers and the kinds of skills required to address the problems brought to the organization by clients and customers. The nature of the encounter deals with the degree to which there is knowledge about cause-effect relationships. Skill specificity refers to the extent to which there is a body of knowledge or techniques and the predictive potential of such knowledge in solving the clients'/customers' problems. In other words, is the service being provided certain to have the intended effects? For example, is the health care provider's efforts certain to reduce the patient's discomfort?

Based on the nature of the encounter and the production and distribution skills required to address client's and customer's problems, a taxonomy of service organizations can be developed. A taxonomy is an analytical tool for classifying organizations in order to better explain and predict how they behave and optimize the use of their resources. For service organizations, such a classification would be based on four critical elements concerning the interaction between the organization and its environment that are reflected in the direct encounter between the service provider and the client or customer (Mills and Margulies 1980):

1. The amount and nature of the information exchanged with the environment;
2. The extent to which the service employee is dependent on clients and customers to provide crucial resources (information). This is reflected by:
   a. the duration of each contact episode or transaction
   b. the likelihood of transaction recurring;
3. The certainty and accuracy of information secured from customers about their needs (i.e., the customer's certainty regarding his or her needs); and
4. The uncertainty surrounding the service provider's skills in addressing customer problems.

Three fundamental types of service organizations can be distinguished: maintenance-interactive, task-interactive, and personal-interactive. These types reflect the encounter between the service organization and customer at the primary operating core or workflow of the organization. The notion of an organization's workflow refers to the area(s) within the organization where the production and distribution of the output occurs. One simple way to tease out the workflow of an organization is to determine the activity that engages the largest number of employees (Pugh, Hickson et al. 1969).

MAINTENANCE-INTERACTIVE SERVICE ORGANIZATIONS

The service organizations within this category are somewhat similar to the distributive services as put forth by Browning and Singlemann (1978). These organizations operate in environments that are perceived to be relatively stable. Examples of maintenance interactive organizations are retail organizations, fast food restaurants, and banking institutions. Relatively little uncertainty surrounds the customer's encounter with the service organization because the resources (information) being exchanged are of a simple nature. The customer is usually very certain about his or her needs or is certain that the organization can provide the services desired. Here the service provider's effort is not so much involved with the production of the service but with the dispensing of it.

Because of the low degree of uncertainty regarding meeting the consumer's demands, specific contracts can be established between the service provider and the customer. Further, the monitoring and enforcement of the terms of the contract can be easily performed.

The limited uncertainty around just how to produce the service makes it more economical for the maintenance service organization to specify in advance responses to consumer demands. Thus, there is a tendency for the organization to standardize activities and set up systems in the operations (Langeard et al., 1981). To ensure efficient system performance, the activities within the encounter must be protected or buffered from outside disruptions or unpredictable activities. Hence, the service provider acts as a boundary spanner in controlling the external environment by restricting the client's/customer's involvement in the exchange to predictable activities. This is quite visible in the encounter between a bank teller and a consumer or the clerk in a fast-food restaurant and a patron in which the demand on the service provider is fairly precise (filling out the deposit slip, making a choice from the menu, etc.). The uncomplicated nature of the customer's problems can often be anticipated and decisions rendered with little reflection by the service provider. It is quite possible to predict customers' activities within these encounters and therefore preplan the organizations' operations. Because the service organization's response to its environment is simplified and the consumer can easily monitor the activities of the service provider, the organization can provide services for a relatively large number of customers.

Further, it is primarily for these reasons that interchangeability occurs among service employees in encounters with customers in maintenance types of organizations. Consequently, transactions within the encounter between the service employee and customers are often limited to social amenities and gracious gestures accompanying the services being dispensed. These may appear to be trivial, but they are of vital importance not only in furthering the flow of information but in determining the customers' satisfaction with the service output.

Usually, the encounter takes very little time for each contact episode and will be repeated frequently over an extended period of time. Although service employees in the maintenance-interactive type services may only briefly interact with customers in each contact episode, most of the employee's total working time is spent in face-to-face interaction with customers. In other words, maintenance service employees interact with many customers for short periods of time.

Maintenance service organizations tend to develop stability with their environments by fostering a sense of loyalty in their customers. The customers will not readily patronize the organization's competitors because a binding relationship—created by necessity, familiarity, or convenience—exists between the organization and the customer. What emerges then between the maintenance service organization and its customers is a relationship that is relatively cosmetic and continuous. Such an association is important for the organization because it fosters what Kurt Lewin calls a large "space of free movement." This means that the maintenance-interactive organization can operate with much more room for planning because its environment changes very slowly and within predictable boundaries allowing the organization to easily adjust. Although there are more small firms in the maintenance-interactive category than large ones, generally the largest service organizations are of the maintenance-interactive type. The relatively stable and simple market environment makes it possible for these organizations to realize scale economies, especially in administration, and take on some of the features of manufacturing organizations in their relationships with their environments. By this we mean that there is much interfirm dependence and much effort directed toward knowing what competitors are doing.

TASK-INTERACTIVE SERVICE ORGANIZATIONS

The task-interactive service organization operates in an environment that is complex with a moderate to high degree of perceived uncertainty. Examples of task-interactive service organizations are legal firms, accounting firms, brokerage organizations, financial institutions, engineering and architectural firms, and marketing and advertising organizations. Here the focus is on the encounter between the service provider and clients/customers and the tasks or skills required to solve the problem or render a service. Thus, the task-interactive service organization refers to the techniques necessary for problemsolving generated by complex environments. Such an organization possesses a body of knowledge that has relatively good predictability and is not generally accessible to the client. Employees are boundary spanners engaged in transformation activities with the environment and as such are not only dispensers of the service but, more significantly, producers also.

The environment of task-interactive service organizations is complex. Although the organization is often in a position to predict important environmental factors by determining the clients' needs, it may not determine the extent to which these needs can be addressed until copious amounts of information have been acquired. In other words, clients entering such encounters are usually quite aware of their problems but lack the expertise to solve them. The client may need, for example, to have a house built. The architect in the service organization may be required to work out the specificity of this service and the extent to which the client's needs can be met within the constraints of the organization's capabilities. The same situation would apply to legal organizations in which a client may require that litigation be brought against another party. But the lawyer would have to work out the details on the feasibility of such a request. There is uncertainty surrounding the solutions to the kinds of problems clients bring to the organization because each problem may be unique. The service provider must possess technical skills and abilities to address such problems in his or her environmental boundary spanning capacity.

There is also uncertainty in the extent to which the client will be completely satisfied after the organization's services are rendered. The complexity required in addressing a client's problems means that much effort can be exerted by the service employee with little success. For example, there is no guarantee that a legal firm will be successful in litigation although it exerted much effort in that endeavor. There are environmental factors beyond the firm's control.

Transactions within encounters of task-interactive service organizations are generally hard to assess because the parties are faced with many contingencies and it is difficult and costly to determine in advance how the parties will respond to these contingencies. The effects of the service provider's effort in providing the service to clients/customers may not be predictable. In such an environment, objective, precise standards cannot be readily imposed. Thus, the contract established between the service provider and client cannot be very precise but will entail a loose set of agreements. Because task-interactive service environments are inherently uncertain, the boundary spanners in these organizations will have to rely on the client's/customer's effort to assist in narrowing the possibilities by providing crucial information. An agreeable contract in terms of tasks to be performed and the nature of the output emerges only after costly negotiations between the service provider and the client. Thus, there is much dependence on clients and customers by service providers in task-interactive service organizations in order for task completion to occur.

The encounter between the task-interactive service organization and the client is a concentrated interaction, each contact episode between the service employee and client lasting for a relatively long duration. The relationship between the service provider and client is not usually continuous but consumated upon completion of the service.

The environment of task-interactive service organizations is not only complex but also dynamic. Environmental dynamism emerges from the interdependence and interrelatedness among competitors. These organizations tend to be relatively small and vulnerable to ease of entry by competitors and failure rate because innovation is readily transferable. Thus, there is much uncertainty created by a competitive environment that requires continuous monitoring.

PERSONAL-INTERACTIVE SERVICE ORGANIZATIONS

Personal-interactive service organizations adjust to their environments by providing what we refer to as personal services to clients and customers. Personal-interactive services are welfare agencies, health care, religious organizations, and psychological consulting or therapy. Historically, it is within this category that the notion of "professionals" and professional organizations emerged. These organizations operate in an environment that is both dynamic and complex. Complexity arises from environmental uncertainty, particularly the tendency of clients and customers to be generally unaware or imprecise, not only about their problems but also about how to go about remedying their problems, as in the case of a patient and his or her health service provider. The service provider will have to direct much effort and skill at diagnosing just what needs to be done. Complexity also emerges from the fact that, in general, there is a lack of complete comprehensibility of the work to be performed for clients and customers. As a boundary spanner, the service employee must possess sophisticated knowledge about clients and customers.

Because uncertainty surrounds both the issues or problems being brought to the organization by clients/customers and the activities necessary to address these issues, the personal-interactive service provider will rely on clients' effort to accomplish their work. To encourage such involvement, the boundary of the organization and its environment has to be broadened. This environmental intrusion into the organization is important to the generation of the service in two areas: problem diagnosis and the nature of the contract.

First, both the service provider and the client/customer must jointly strive to determine what the client's problems or wants may actually be. Clients are required to provide information to the service worker so that some diagnosis can be made. Much of this information is of a personal or confidential nature. This type of boundary spanning search activity would be too costly to undertake without the direct input by the client. A further complication in the search activity is the tendency for each contact episode to be different and consequently to generate different sets of problems. For example, each time a patient sees his or her health care provider there is a new set of issues to address. It is for this reason that the search and diagnostic activity is an ongoing process.

The other reason for relying on the client's effort in personal-interactive encounters involves the nature of the contract. Within personal-interactive services, contracts are established on the basis of occupations rather than tasks (Friedson 1973). The abilities and skills necessary to address the problems of clients and customers are of a relatively general nature and are acquired from general training, that is, training from a wide exposure of knowledge. The body of knowledge or techniques that exists for dealing with environmental uncertainty is very much devoid of predictive power. Thus, the cause-effect relationship between what the service employee does and the outcome from such action is not very sound. For example, there is little guarantee that the welfare counselor's efforts in assisting the recipient to be self-sufficient will succeed. This is also true for the actions taken by a psychiatrist in trying to improve the well-being of a schizophrenic client. The limited predictability of the knowledge in these personal-interactive encounters is at least partially attributable to the tendency of clients and customers within these encounters to be reactive in the exchange of information. What works in rendering the service with one client may not be effective for others, and what works even in one contact episode with a particular client may not work in other episodes with the same client. In a real sense, the service providers are investigators looking for clues, especially during diagnosis. Consequently, there is a demand for creativity and frequent novelty as the service provider's techniques become idiosyncratic or situational. Further, the situational nature of each contact episode requires novel solutions of a largely judgmental nature.

Generally, the complexity of such environmental encounters renders the contracts between the service employee and clients necessarily incomplete. It is extremely difficult and costly to specify contractually how much energy the service provider is to devote to a complex task. Since the service provider's performance cannot be costlessly contracted upon, there is much temptation for opportunism. The service provider will be tempted to shirk his or her responsibilities.

The potential for opportunism increases the client's role in these interactions. Clients will have to become actively involved in the monitoring and policing of the service provider in order to ensure that there is no breach or violation of the loosely established agreement in providing the service. Again, the boundary of the organization has to be permeable in order to entertain such client activities.

The clients' monitoring activities are often reduced by various bonding mechanisms by the service provider. One such mechanism centers around the reputation of the service provider. The notion of reputation signals to others the service provider's credibility. His or her reputation is particularly important because clients of the personal-interactive encounters do not generally perceive themselves as qualified to evaluate the services being rendered. The complexity of the activities suggests that only service providers and their colleagues are capable of evaluating the services provided and the competence of the providers. In a sense, these clients are quite vulnerable. Primarily because of this factor an aura of professionalism is often established around the personal-interactive service encounters so that the service provider's peers or colleagues can perform some of the monitoring activities for clients (Blau and Scott 1962). Professionalism protects clients by increasing their confidence in the service provider. It further serves as a method for weeding out those who could most likely do damage to clients and customers.

Within the personal-interactive service organization, clients will generally interact or be served by one service employee or a designated team until the service is complete. Substitutability of employees in their interaction with clients and customers is held to a minimum, as each contact episode affects and is affected by others. The rationale for this is based on the personal nature of the information that clients are required to provide to the service employee. In order for the client to divulge such sensitive information, trust in the service employee is required. In other words, the service employee must build a relationship with the client so that the latter will feel comfortable providing such intimate and often crucial information. The establishment of such relationships is often time consuming since it requires much interaction between the service employee and client.

Also contributing to the uncertainty of the personal-interactive service organizations is the competitive environment that is stimulated by a large number of small firms. There is a preponderance of small organizations providing personal-interactive services, and their interdependence generates instability in the market environment.

SUMMARY

The environment is important to the performance of organizations because of its effect on the kinds of decisions that are made within the firm. For the service firm, the direct impact crucial environmental elements have on the operations of services make environment immensely significant. Service organizations are more directly dependent on the clients/customers for the performance of their task activities. What emerges between the service firm and the environment are contracts with clients/customers in which mutually beneficial agreements are established around the generation of the service output.

A typology based on the relationship with the clients/customers in the environment classifies service organizations as maintenance-interactive, task-interactive, and professional-interactive. Classifying service organizations is important because it provides a general set of principles for explaining the behavior of these firms. By combining

many variables into a simple constant, classification facilitates dealing with the complexity of these organizations and predicting future
behaviors and certain patterns of relationships of organizations that
fall into each category. Since each category reflects the nature of the
environments's intrusion into the operations of the organization, we
would expect such intrusions to have an effect on the functioning
of major elements of these firms. An important element in the
operation of services is technology. The next chapter will examine
the effects of client/customer intrusion on the functioning of this
element.

3 THE TECHNOLOGY OF SERVICE ORGANIZATIONS

An important element in the operation of organizations is their technology. The technology of organizations is a difficult concept to pinpoint because it implies different things to different people. It is therefore not surprising that there is much confusion among both practicing managers and writers about exactly what the technology of an organization is. There is general agreement, however, that technology is a complex element crucial to the production of goods and services.

One simple approach to understanding technology in service organizations is from an input-output framework (Emery and Trist 1965). An organization survives by incorporating certain types of material from its environment. This material, which may take the form of raw material, people, symbols, information, and so on, is transformed and exported back to the environment as finished goods and services. In a sense, technology is the transformation of things coming into the service organization into things going out. Technology is how the service organization gets done what needs to be done in solving problems. It entails all of the activities and techniques involved in the conversion of the input into output.

To most managers technology is a major source for increasing their organization's productivity. Although productivity gains can be realized by motivating people to produce more, the results are far less impressive than those that technology can generate.

Technology is also important because it determines, to a large degree, the jobs that people perform in organizations. This role is quite visible in many service organizations where technology and machines have changed the nature of work. For example, the introduction of automatic teller machines (ATMs) in banks has replaced low-skilled jobs (tellers) and placed more emphasis on high-skilled jobs (programmers, loan officers, etc.). Further, technology influences the way people are organized or structured, the types of social interactions people engage in, people's attitudes about their organizations, and the behaviors they display (Litterer 1965).

Clearly, technology is important in the functioning of service organizations. In order to capture the dynamics of technology it is necessary to examine how the technical system interacts with other parts of an organization.

Organizations, whether services or manufacturing, are cooperative systems that are deliberate and purposeful. Inherent in this cooperation among people is the division of labor, where work is segmented into task activities among the participants. But for these segmented activities to be purposeful they must also be integrated. Thus, within service organizations there exists a complex interdependence of people's task activities. The technical system emerges as the "collective instruments" employed by the participants in performing their task activities (Hunt 1970). This implies that the task activities or duties of people in organizations are essentially "problem loaded," and the extent to which solutions to these problems can be generated is largely dependent on the employee. It thus follows that technology is more realistically perceived as direct problemsolving intervention in a somewhat organized way. Put more simply, service organizations are rational or deliberate instruments that synthesize the skills of their members.

COMPLEXITY OF SERVICE OPERATIONS

A service (i.e., an effort or a performance) is not accomplished alone but is rendered by the service employee to clients and customers. Thus, services entail doing something for someone who is unable, unwilling, or incapable of doing it for him- or herself. The contract that is established between the service provider and the client/customer is primarily concerned with what the provider will do for the client recipient and the expectations about what will be done. From this perspective, the technology is the product of service organizations (Fitzsimons and Sullivan 1982). In other words, the technology is the service being rendered by the service provider to clients/customers. It is the inseparability of the service being rendered to the client/customer from the technology within the service organization's operations that increases the complexity of the production function of these organizations.

Unlike that of manufacturing output, the production of the service output emerges from a social situation; a transaction between the service employee and clients and customers. Within such transactions clients and customers become integral parts of the service organization technology because it is difficult to separate them from the input (information raw material) they provide to the production process of service operations. This is so irrespective of whether the customer inputs through an ATM or a patient interacts directly with his or her physician. As a result, clients and customers will have an impact on the transformation systems of service operations, the extent of which is dependent on the type of encounter at the workflow.

An interesting way to demonstrate the activities of service operations is to apply the well-known input-output model mentioned earlier. Within this formulation the transformation system consists of a logical sequence of events or set of activities as shown in Figure 3–1. First there is an input subsystem, which entails raw materials or information from the external environment. The input material passes into a conversion subsystem where the "core" technologies ex-

Figure 3–1. Service Workflow Transformation.

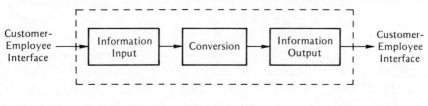

Transformation Process

ist and are applied to add value to the raw material. As a result of the activities in the conversion subsystems, there is an output of finished goods and services. Conceptualizing service operations in this framework is valuable because it demonstrates that the interdependence of the input, conversion, and output subsystems, and it subjects the activities in these processes to degrees of rationalization. This framework has been used primarily to depict the operations of manufacturing organizations in which the potential to rationalize activities is mainly due to the absence of the clients'/customers' direct involvement in the production function. This framework is relevant to service organizations in which the direct involvement of clients and customers can be effectively removed from the service operations. However, when clients and customers are directly involved in the production process of services, the input-output framework becomes more complex, as Figure 3-2 shows.

Daniel Bell (1973) has observed that manufacturing organizations work on things and service organizations work on people. This has important implications for service operations. Figure 3-2 shows that service operations that involve direct client and customer encounters employ technologies not only in the conversion process but also in the input and output. Because clients and customers are potentially reactive raw materials when they enter the service operations, it is possible that they may find solutions to some or even all of their service problems within input and output subsystems. For example, the ambiance in a bank as customers wait in queues and the facilities in restaurants may contribute greatly not only to the bundle of services produced and consumed but also to the technologies employed in the production. From this perspective, the notion of technology is applicable at all phases of the transformation process. Indeed, each stage of the transformation system—that is, input, conversion, and output—may require a unique set of techniques or technology.

Another important factor that increases the complexity of the service operations when clients and customers are directly involved concerns the way services are produced within this context. Client and customer encounters with service operations make the production of the service output a transaction or social interaction wherein the transformation process fosters the skipping of stages (e.g., low insurance risks are permitted to waive exams) and even the premature termination of the service before it is fully rendered (e.g., litigants may engage in out-of-court settlements). It is for this reason

Figure 3-2. A Systems Model of the Service Production Process.

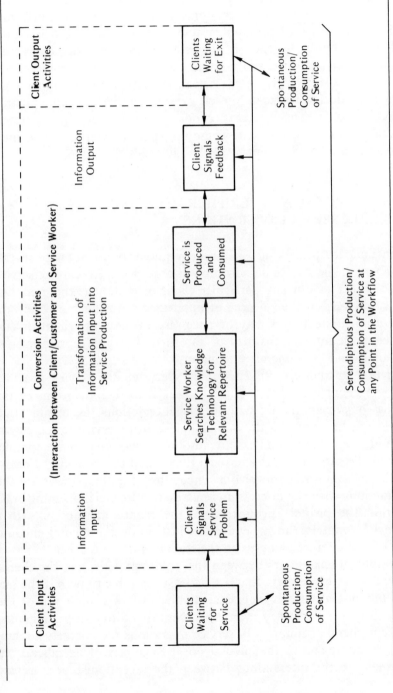

Source: P. Mills and D. Moberg, "Perspectives on the Technology of Service Operations," *Academy of Management Review* ⁻ (1982), pp. 467–478.

that, although the transformation process may comprise several typical information-exchange subsystems, as we have indicated in Figure 3-2, the sequence of these subsystems is more of a reciprocal nature rather than linear. Further, it is possible that unintended or serendipitous conversions or satisfaction by clients and customers may occur at any stage in the transformation system. For example, a patient may decide to treat himself after an initial encounter with a physician, or a consumer may choose to do her own taxes after a meeting with an accountant. These unexpected eventualities cannot be readily predicted except by probability models.

PIVOTAL AND PERIPHERAL ENCOUNTERS IN SERVICE OPERATIONS

Clients and customers may often be required to interact with several members of the service organization in order for the complete service to be rendered. For any particular client or customer, these interactions will vary in their degree of importance. Although a wide variety of such encounters may be necessary for any one client or customer, these interactions may be categorized into two basic groups: "pivotal" and "peripheral" encounters.

Pivotal encounters are encounters between the service provider and the client/customer that are so crucial to the operations of the service organization that without the interactions the organization would not be providing the minimally adequate service to the client/customer. Pivotal encounters are absolutely necessary to the completion of the task activities and form the core of the exchange. For example, in a hospital the pivotal encounters for the patient are the interactions with the doctors and nurses; in a financial planning organization the pivotal encounters are the client's interaction with a financial counselor; in an education institution the pivotal encounters are the interaction between the student and the teacher.

Peripheral encounters between the service provider and the client/customer are encounters that are at least desirable to permit the service but not absolutely necessary to the overall completion of the task activities. They may even involve entirely different participants. The peripheral encounters in service operations serve largely to support or complement the pivotal ones. Examples of peripheral encounters are the interactions between the receptionist or secretary and the client in a legal organization, the interaction between the student and the personnel in the registrar's office in an education institution, and the interaction between the x-ray technician and the patient in health care institution. Generally, the more peripheral encounters the client/customer engages in, the smoother will be the performance of the service operations. Since both pivotal and peripheral encounters entail the exchange of resources between clients/customers and the service provider, the fundamental elements of the transformation system—input, conversion, output—will be inherent in these encounters.

Clearly, the technologies in the operations of services are complicated by the direct involvement of clients and customers within these systems, irrespective of whether such encounters are pivotal or peripheral. The reciprocal nature of the transactions in the encounters between clients and customers and service workers is a fundamental unit of the production process. This in turn suggests that the technology within this context may indeed vary not only across service organizations but even across the phases of the transformation system within a particular service organization.

TYPES OF TECHNOLOGY IN
SERVICE OPERATIONS

In general, the notion of technology in service operations implies techniques in some order and pattern to solve problems. Such problemsolving techniques can be grouped into two fundamental types: machine technology and knowledge technology (Dubin 1968). Machine technology comprises all of the tools, instruments, machines, and technological formulas essential to the performance of the work. It lends itself to processes and systems where output can be easily monitored to ensure compliance with specifications. Machine technology is applicable to those service operations in which the clients'/customers' requests are relatively simple in nature and are recurring. Thus, the contract established between the client/customer and the service provider can be specific with very little uncertainty—for example, the use of ATMs in banks.

Knowledge technology, on the other hand, entails the set of ideas responsible for expressing the goals of the work and the importance of and rationale for the techniques used by the service provider.

Knowledge technologies are used when contracts between the service provider and clients/customers cannot be specified in detail and are of a general nature. Thus, the techniques of knowledge technology do not lend themselves to predictable situations and are applicable to unstable and complex environments that generate client/customer problems that are uncertain, unique, and unpredictable. An example of knowledge technology is the skills required of a physician to address the patient's problems.

TECHNOLOGY IN LOW-ENCOUNTER SERVICES

We noted in Chapter 2 that the environment of low-encounter services (maintenance-interactive services such as banks and retail organizations) is stable and of a simple nature. The contracts established between the service provider and clients/customers are relatively specific. There is a clear understanding not only of what the client/customer requests but also of the expectations of just how such services will be rendered. The specificity of contracts in low-contact services reduces the necessity for clients'/customers' direct interaction with the service provider. Thus, customer involvement in the operations is relatively limited, and many service organizations in these predictable environments have further reduced customer involvement and uncertainty by removing these participants from the service operations (e.g., employing ATMs in banks) or restricting their participation to a specific set of activities. When customer involvement in service operations is low or limited, the organizations can perform as relatively closed systems. By restricting environmental influences, the service organization can insulate or protect its core technologies. It is then in a better position to rationalize its activities.

A service organization can seal off its core technologies by surrounding them with input and output mechanisms. Thompson (1967) has noted that these mechanisms can take the following forms:

1. *Filtering* inputs into the service operations—for example, restricting the kinds of clients/customers the organization will serve;
2. *Stocking*—having adequate facilities, equipment, and employees on hand for customers—for example, enough rooms on hand for hotel customers;

3. *Preparing*—for example, training employees so that they are capable of offering the services needed by customers;
4. *Smoothing*—providing incentives to interested parties in the environment so that fluctuations in supply and demand can be reduced—for example, reducing the price of the service during off-peak periods; and
5. *Rationing*—restricting the service to a selected few when demands exceed the supply—for example, hospitals accepting only critical patients during an emergency.

When a service organization can effectively seal off its core technology, it can perform as a closed system, and in so doing, the organization can expect little disruption from the external environment. In these types of services, both workflow and task uncertainty are low. Workflow uncertainty means the degree to which the service organization can predict the customers arrival and exit patterns over time. One would expect workflow uncertainty to be relatively low where appointment schedules can be established in order to predict and plan for clients' and customers' arrival into the service operations.

Workflow uncertainty can also be low when the service organization can determine the peak periods when customers will place heavy demands on its operations, as in a fast food restaurant. Conversely, workflow uncertainty would be high when the service organization is unable to predict when clients and customers will enter into its operations. For example, we would expect high workflow uncertainty in the emergency operations of a hospital or in a fire department.

Task uncertainty refers to a lack of knowledge about how to accomplish the service outcomes. When the task activities are well understood and the cause-effect relationship is clear, then the uncertainty surrounding such activities will be low. Conversely, when activities for problemsolving are nebulous and the cause-effect relationship unclear, there is much uncertainty for the organization (Slocum and Simms 1980).

The presence of low task uncertainty suggests that the organization is able to predict the nature of the customers' problems and the techniques necessary to address these problems. Consequently, the organization can preplan for these activities. Further, low task uncertainty means that the techniques to solve customers' problems are relatively simple and can be readily rationalized.

Here, the low-contact or low-encounter service organization can effectively divide its operations into a back office and a front office dimension (Chase 1978).The activities of the back office operations can be buffered from direct customer involvement, making it possible for the organization to realize efficiencies by sequencing its problemsolving activities (Chase and Tansik 1982). In other words, systems and processes can be established to provide relatively standardized services. The efficiency of such systems is not only dependent on the low-uncertainty task activities but also on how well the organization can predict when the customer will enter and leave its operations, that is, workflow uncertainty.

The front office operations entail the service employee's directly interacting with the consumer. But front office activities are directly related to what occurs in the back office operations, so some predictability of what occurs between the customer and the service employee must be achieved in order for the systems established in the back office to function efficiently. The low-contact service organization will restrict the activities of both the service employee and the customer. One way the organization does this is by clearly indicating to the customer the kinds of services being offered and specifically what the customer is expected to do in the interaction. It is perhaps more accurate to view the employees in these encounters with customers as dispensers of the service rather than producers of it.

For low-contact service organizations where operations are explicit and easy to replicate, high-volume machine technologies or procedures can be implemented with detailed standard operating procedures for back office personnel and for employees and customers in the encounter to follow. This is clearly visible in, for example, fast food restaurants and banks. In both the back and front office areas there is machine-type sequencing of activities, with detailed specificity for the evaluation of the operations, which affords workflow continuity. The repetition inherent in production procedures ensures the elimination of imperfection in technology by increasing the possibility for spotting redundancies and other potential malfunctions. From this perspective the technological process helps to control the activities within the operations.

TECHNOLOGY IN HIGH-ENCOUNTER SERVICES

High-encounter service organizations (task-interactive and personal-interactive services) operate in complex environments. Consequently, uncertainty surrounds the comprehensibility of the activities involved in the production of services. These organizations are required to secure quantities of sophisticated information and knowledge about their clients and customers, and much of this required information is obtained directly from clients and customers themselves by means of their heavy involvement in the organizations' operations.

When clients and customers must become deeply involved in the operations of services, sealing off the core technologies of these organizations cannot be readily accomplished. In other words, the relatively complex involvement of clients and customers prevents these organizations from operating their core technologies as closed systems. It is therefore very difficult to separate the operating core into back office activities and front office activities. Instead, high-encounter organizations must operate as more open systems in which the environment is directly brought into all facets of the transformation system by the relatively complex nature of clients' and customers' demands. Some high-encounter services such as public accounting firms seem to have isolated the core operations fairly well. These are unique situations because the service providers go to the clients and not vice versa.

High-encounter service organizations require technologies with a relatively large capacity for information processing within the transformation system. This is clearly visible in relationships between, for example, health care providers and their clients and customers. Much of this information is of an equivocal nature and thus subject to various interpretations.

Each contact episode between the service worker and a client/customer creates a "decision unit" (Duncan 1972). It is within the decision unit that much of the transformation system resides in that the critical elements in the production of the service are the gathering and processing of information. These activities must occur before the actual service output is rendered to clients and customers. In a very real sense, the data-gathering phase of the production process subordinates the actual conversion or service rendered. This is because the more accurate and reliable the information received from the clients and customers, the easier it is for the service employee to diagnose and transform such information.

The relatively active involvement of clients and customers in high-encounter service operations increases the complexity of the technologies in another way. Bringing clients and customers into the operations is an attempt by the organization to reduce environmental uncertainty, a way of co-opting an uncertain environmental element (Thompson and McEwen 1958). By entering fully into the operations of high-contact service organizations, clients and customers are required to adhere to some guidelines and procedures and are thus potentially under the influence of the organization. Yet, the presence of clients and customers in service operations creates uncertainty for the efficiency with which these systems can function. This is primarily because clients/customers are reactive. In each contact episode clients/customers are, to a great extent, ego involved in the production process; it is they or their personal property that is being transformed. This situation creates high risks for the effectiveness of systems, simply because such reactivity will produce consequences that cannot be readily anticipated with any meaningful measure of regularity.

It is largely due to the heavy client and customer involvement in high-encounter service operations and the uncertainty they generate to the necessary task activities that these organizations are required to use knowledge technologies. Service workers in high-encounter operations cannot rely on past procedures, methods, and ways of doing their jobs since workers are continually being confronted with novel situations that require unique techniques (Emergy and Trist 1965; Terreberry 1968). In order to successfully perform their activities, these service providers have to possess much knowledge and a wide repertoire of skills capable of generating solutions to unique situations. Consequently, the technology for high-encounter service operations is more accurately viewed as situation specific. In other words, this is "bit-service technology" because not only is it situation specific but it can be adjusted to accommodate the different phases of the transformation system (input, conversion, or output) to clients'/customers' needs, whether this entails shortening the service at the input phase (e.g., a client decides to design her house after the initial meeting with the architect) or skipping phases in the process (e.g., no medical check-up for some insurance clients).

One reason that the technology of high-encounter services is increasingly troublesome for the service organization is that it is difficult to monitor. Standards cannot be established against which output can be uniformly evaluated. Consequently, the employee emerges as an independent decision unit required to have skills and knowledge in several organizational functions. Such employees are not only involved in the production of the service but must also simultaneously market these services to the client/customer. Further, they must also manage the client/customer by motivating him or her to provide the crucial information raw material required to deliver the service. In sum, the application of bit-service technology is necessary because the service employee has to acquire techniques that can address issues in production, marketing, and personnel functions in order to perform effectively in high-encounter service operations.

THE ACTIVITIES OF CLIENTS AND CUSTOMERS

When clients and customers are directly involved in the operations of services, they become an integral part of the technology. Thus, services emerge from the coordinated efforts of both service employees and clients and customers. This suggests that clients and customers have important task activities to perform within the operations of services (Bateson 1985; Langeard et al. 1981). Such activities are quite clear, for example, when a bank customer fills out a deposit slip, a customer in a retail store selects and takes the goods to the checkout counter, or a patient monitors and relates symptoms to the physician.

Service delivery systems often require clients to perform activities by conforming to certain behavioral standards that allow the service operations to function smoothly and efficiently. These activities may extend to all stages of the transformation process.

On the input side, clients and customers can perform many task activities. Before entering into the operations of services, clients and customers can acquire some of the knowledge used in the creation of the service. For example, sick people can consult reference books so that they can prediagnose their ailments. This can be invaluable to the physician because the more symptoms the client provides the more accurate the diagnosis.

In the conversion phase, clients may be required to process information by actually choosing among alternatives. Such decisionmaking requirements are typical in retail organizations and restaurants, where patrons are expected to choose among alternative items, or in self-help health care, where patients are expected to assist in the treatment. Such participation would support the point that technical involvement by clients and customers may indeed be an integral part of the conversion subsystem in service operations.

On the output side of the transformation system, clients and customers may be required to perform task activities after they have departed the workflow, that is, outside of direct, personal, face-to-face contact with the service employee. Task activities in the form of postoperative exercises may be required of the patient; clients may be required to develop and maintain a system of record keeping for their meeting with the tax accountant the following year.

THE TECHNOLOGY OF MONITORING IN SERVICE OPERATIONS

One of the paramount reasons that clients/customers become directly involved in the operations of services involves the contracts established with the service provider. In the exchange between the client/customer and service provider, both parties may attempt to maximize their resources. This means that the client/customer attempts to secure the most effort from the service provider, and the provider attempts to secure as much money or other rewards as possible from the client/customer with the least effort possible. Within this context of resource maximization, the service provider may be tempted to shirk his or her responsibilities or engage in opportunistic behaviors. In order to protect their interests and ensure that the contract is fulfilled, clients/customers are required to monitor the service provider's activities. The extent to which they must do so is a function of the contract. When the contract is specific, the client/customer will exert relatively little effort in monitoring the service provider's activities. Conversely, when contracts are difficult to specify then relatively more monitoring effort will be exerted.

In a low-contact service operation, the effort and expectations from the service provider are unequivocal. Consequently, it is relatively simple for the client/customer to monitor and examine the service outcome. For example, when a customer patronizes a fast food restaurant and orders a hamburger, the outcome can easily be observed and much of the process too. The customer knows what to expect because the contract specifies some standard for a desirable hamburger. Further, the customer need not become involved in the back-office operations because he or she can evaluate the outcome against some predetermined standard and detect deviations in expected outcomes. Thus, for the customer, control is being exercised by output activities. The situation is quite different for the high-contact service operation. For these service encounters the contract established between the client and the service provider cannot be very specific because of the uncertainty surrounding the service to be rendered. Since there is uncertainty around not only the activities in the production of the service but also the eventual service outcome, standards cannot be readily established. For example, good medical care or the rendering of proper legal service is very difficult to define, and therefore contracts cannot be specific. Consequently, there is a relatively greater potential for the service provider to engage in opportunistic behavior, that is, to violate the essence of the contract. It is also more difficult for the client to monitor the service provider's activities.

The monitoring activities required of clients in high-contact services will not focus on the output, as one would find in a low-contact service operation. Instead, the client's efforts will concentrate on the service provider's process or production activities. This is because the services produced from high-contact interactions are generally irreversible. Once a ruling on a litigation case is rendered or the advice of one's financial adviser is acted upon, there is little the client can do to affect that particular service. New contracts will have to be established for new services. For this reason, clients will have to become actively involved in the actual activities being performed by the service provider. This involvement may take the form of doing some of the work by asking pertinent questions, seeking second opinions, or becoming astute about activities that would be reasonable in the rendering of that particular service.

It is within this context that the use of knowledge technology by the service provider is crucial. As clients attempt to protect their self-interest by monitoring the service provider's task activities, the service provider will have to justify why certain activities and techniques are being employed. Much explanation as to the rationale for the goals or outcome of the service and the technology used in this outcome will have to be given to the client in order to satisfy the latter's contract expectations.

It seems clear that in the transformation system of service organizations clients and customers are direct participants in the technology. And although they may not actually participate actively in all three phases of the transformation process—input, conversion, and output—rarely can they escape performing some task activities in at least one phase.

SUMMARY

This chapter showed the difficulties of examining service technologies, particularly when clients and customers are actively involved in the operations. Service technology often involves clients/customers in all phases of the transformation system. This is not the case in the manufacturing context where relatively more buffering of core technologies can be achieved for efficiency.

The technology of service operations is problematic because it cannot be readily separated from the service output. Service organizations are essentially engaged in selling technology to their clients/customers. This gives rise to the notion that service technology is a social phenomenon that emerges from the interaction between the clients/customers and the service provider. It is within this interaction that vital information for producing the service is exchanged. As such, service technology is largely knowledge-based rather than machine-based.

Clients/customers are crucial to service operations, and the degree to which they become involved in the operations (i.e., the technology) is dependent on the nature of the service demands and the contract established. An important issue for service firms is how to optimize client/customer involvement in the technology of service operations. This issue can be dealt with meaningfully by the relationship between technology and other properties of the service firm. A related property that affects the client's/customer's involvement in service operations is the design or structure of the organization. The next chapter will explore the relationship between technology and how service organizations segment and coordinate their work-related activities.

4 FACTORS THAT AFFECT DESIGN PARAMETERS OF SERVICE ORGANIZATIONS

We observed earlier that organizations import resources from their environment, convert them into some output, and export them back into their environment. The productivity of the firm is directly related to the costs incurred from these operating activities. In a market environment, the more cost efficient an organization is relative to prices, the higher its survival potential.

Two broad categories of costs are affiliated with the operating activities within service firms: operating costs and organizing costs. Operating costs are explicit costs that are outlays made by the organization and are generally considered to be accounting expenses — for example, selling and administrative expenses, taxes, depreciation, cost depletion and retirements, interest and debt expenses, payments for rent, maintenance and repairs, payroll, material and supplies.

Organizing costs, on the other hand, are the expenses incurred from the internal governance of the organization. These are implicit costs emerging from the manner in which human assets are organized. Organizing costs have traditionally been overlooked in computing the expenses of firms and are quite different from operating costs. Unlike the operating costs, organizing costs do not entail an "expense" outlay (Leftwich 1966), but methods of allocating and controlling resources by consensus (Williamson 1975). In essence, organizing costs are expenses connected with the structuring of

53

organizations. Such expenses may emerge from several sources, especially when there is a great deal of overlap and interaction among organization departments. For example, a marketing analyst may be required to work closely with the purchasing and advertising departments. But it may not be clearly defined as to who is responsible for what activities. Organizing costs may result from the duplication of effort, tasks not being performed because one group assumed the other group had taken care of it, conflicts between the two groups, etc.

One of the major decisions facing service organization managers is how to organize or structure people and their activities in the most cost-effective way. "Organizing" something in essence refers to the structuring, coordinating, or controlling of that thing. Thus, organization and structure may be synonymous in that each implies a particular arrangement or composition of activities in some ordered fashion.

Structure is a very elusive concept because it is abstract at first glance. Structure is difficult to see, feel, or touch. We can, however, picture an organization's structure by examining just what it is supposed to do. Adopting this approach, we find that structure entails a framework that facilitates the efficient operation of the various processes (e.g., communication, authority, control, decision-making), which in turn directly contributes to the operating activities. Thus, structure seeks to give some order to the activities occurring within the firm by optimizing the use of resources within the organization.

DIFFERENTIATION OF ACTIVITIES

One of the fundamental principles of work in organizations is the division of labor, or the differentiation of work into task activities with each organization member being responsible for a discrete set of activities. Yet each member's set of activities is intricately linked to other aspects or activities. There is an interdependence of all the activities performed by the participants. Consequently, as Mintzberg (1979) notes, structure can be summarized as the ways an organization segments its work into discrete activities (e.g., in an accounting firm the division of labor could take the form of consulting, tax auditing, or government contracts) and at the same time coordinates these activities.

The structure of an organization then consists of parts that become indirectly observable in some physical arrangement and are bound together. It may be more meaningful to view the parts of a structure as events because they are activities actually performed by people. Thus, structure emerges as a set of interrelated events and indeed revolves around events and not merely around the arrangement of things (Allport 1962). Within this context, the structure of organizations, particularly service organizations, is an interweaving of human interaction and all of the coordination mechanisms into patterned relationships in order to accomplish some intended goal.

Because structure is basically a set of relationships, it involves an inherently interpersonal element. It is this interpersonal element rather than its interpositional element that renders the structure of organizations dynamic. The link between the interpositional and interpersonal can be complex and is particularly crucial for service organizations, which tend to be labor intensive.

The interaction of these structural elements may become clearer by examining how people behave in organizations. When employees become members of service organizations, they occupy positions or roles and each position is attached to other positions to form a role set. Thus, people in these positions have complex interactions with people in other positions. Such interpersonal interactions will tend to be distinct or unique because people bring personal idiosyncracies, attitudes, needs, and expectations to their positions. When positions in organizations are changed through turnover or promotion, the new occupant enters the position with a new set of attitudes, needs, expectations, and idiosyncracies that directly affect the relationships among the organization members. Consequently, it is not the position per se that makes structure interesting but the interpersonal interactions (Allport 1962; Litterer 1965).

DIMENSIONS OF STRUCTURE

Although the structure of organizations is a continuous process, it is helpful to address structure by its most common dimensions. When we refer to the dimensions of structure, we mean attributes that are present in all organizations. The most salient dimensions of structure are:

1. *Standardization*—the extent to which there is a set of procedures for dealing with regularly occurring activities;
2. *Formalization*—the extent to which there are written rules and regulations for people to follow;
3. *Specialization*—the degree to which labor is broken down into discrete activities;
4. *Centralization*—the degree to which the authority within the organization is concentrated at the top;
5. *Configuration*—the shape and form of the organization, for example, the span of control of the chief executive, the span of control of the first line supervisor, the number of levels in management hierarchy, the number of supervisors to nonsupervisors; and
6. *Flexibility*—the ability or degree to which the organization can adjust its internal parts to adapt to changes occurring in the external market (Puch, Hickson et al. 1969).

What then gives organizations their unique design is the degree to which these dimensions are present in various arrangements.

DESIGN AND DECISIONMAKING

The dimensions of structure outlined in the preceding section exist primarily to determine how decisions are made within the service organization. Essentially, the design or structure of service organizations is concerned with who makes what decisions and how decisions are made. Thus, the dimensions of structure address the organization's decisionmaking process and the degree of employee involvement in this process.

The association between the design and the decisionmaking process within an organization is based on the notion of authority. Authority means to control or to add form to something. Thus, authority in organizations adds form to the organization or regulates its activities. Consequently, the authority structure is the governance mechanism of organizations.

The notion of authority in organizations can be defined as the right or ability to make decisions for others as to what activities they should perform, how they should perform these activities, and when they should undertake such activities (Simon 1957; Dubin 1958). From this perspective, authority emerges as a limited class of decisions in which one establishes rules to govern the behavior of other members within the organization. Two types of limited classes of decisions are readily discernible. Policy-type decisions (e.g., credit policy, credit risk) are made on the higher levels. Tactical-type decisions are made at the lower levels of the service firm. These decisions center around the interaction with clients/customers and the authority afforded the service employees to perform their tasks with some discretion. The decisionmaking process links authority with organization structure. Thus, when reference is made to the structure or the design of organizations, it is essentially a reference to the decisionmaking process and the degree to which the members within the organization participate in this process.

As an important dimension of structure, the decisionmaking process has several fundamental phases. Fama and Jensen (1983) isolate four. First, there is the "initiation," during which ideas, proposals, and alternatives are generated for the optimum use of the organization's resources. Second is the "ratification," which entails choosing among the decision initiatives for implementation. The third phase is the "implementation," where the ratified or actual choice that has been made is put into practice. Finally, there is the "monitoring" phase, in which the performance of those implementing the ratified decisions is evaluated, measured, or scrutinized.

It is possible to separate the phases in the decisionmaking process into decision management and decision control. In decision management the employee initiates and implements the decisions. In decision control there is not only ratification of the decision initiated but also the monitoring of such decisions.

To a large degree, then, the way that service organizations are governed or structured is a function of how the factors of decision control and decision management are distributed. In other words, the form or design of the organization will be determined by who within the organization becomes involved in the decision management and decision control. Further, the nature of the design will be determined by the extent to which these factors can be readily separated in order to optimize the use of resources, particularly in the direct exchanges with clients and customers.

FACTORS THAT INFLUENCE THE DESIGN
OF SERVICE ORGANIZATIONS

For the manager concerned with the design of service organizations, an important issue is how to arrange the relationships or establish the composition of the workforce in such a way that there is optimum use of resources. In order to accomplish this, the manager must contend with two basic causal problems, which are necessarily sequential. The first has to do with certification (decision management) and the other with inspection (decision control) (Weick 1976).

In certification, the manager decides which members will actually perform the task activities or implement ratified decisions. Decisions must be made about who will interface with clients and customers and who will not, who will be involved in pivotal and relevant encounters with clients/customers and who will not.

Equally important is the problem of inspection. Here the manager is concerned with the performance of those involved in the task activities and the extent to which there is adherence to agreed upon standards, both implicit and explicit. Contractual arrangements exist within service organizations, for example, between the service organization and its employees or between the organization and its clients/customers. Such agreements, especially as they pertain to the exchanges between the service provider and the client/customer, have to be monitored to ensure that the proper services are being rendered. In order to address these issues of certification and inspection, it is necessary to examine factors that are likely to influence the structure of service organizations.

Many factors may affect the internal arrangement of human assets within service organizations, including the age and size of the organization, strategy, what is fashionable, and even the decisionmakers' choices or the whims of the manager. Perhaps the most widely recognized elements impacting on the organization of human assets are technology and the environment.

TECHNOLOGICAL DETERMINISM

As noted earlier, one of the major problems with which organizations have to contend is that of certification or who does the actual task activities within the division of labor context. This "doing" perspective to organization structure seems to have been the rationale behind the widely held proposition that the structure of organizations is dependent on technology. In other words, organizations have a form of technological determinism.

The idea that the design of organizations is determined by the technology or what people do has been held by both practicing managers and writers in management for over eight decades. Economist Thorstein Veblen (1904) pointed out that modern technology was the dominant element in the operations of an organization and impacted significantly on all segments of organizations. Dubin (1959) went further by stating that technology is the most important single determinant of working behavior in organizations. Much empirical work spanning three decades has been conducted on the relationship between the design of an organization and its technology. In general, these studies offer strong support of the notion that the way an organization is structured is largely dependent on the nature of the technology.

An important caveat should be noted regarding the studies examining the relationship between technology and structure. When these studies set up a service-manufacturing dichotomy, the relationship between technology and structure becomes less clear. Studies that were conducted on manufacturing organizations indicate conclusive support that technology influences structure in these organizations. However, studies of the relationship between technology and structure in service organizations have found inconsistent support (Mills and Moberg 1982).

The strong empirical findings that technology influences structure in manufacturing organizations should not surprise us. The operations of manufacturing organizations lend themselves more readily to what J.D. Thompson (1967) calls norms of organization rationality. Under norms of rationality, organizations seek to seal off or protect their core technologies. This reduces uncertainty and thus facilitates the application of closed system logic, as earlier argued. System techniques are more readily applicable when uncertainty can be reduced or controlled. Within the manufacturing context, the raw material worked on is tangible so lends itself more readily to cause-effect relationships and the manipulation of the production process to varying degrees of predictability. The participants can be arranged in such a way as to facilitate the optimum performance of the productive techniques. Consequently, the organization can deindividualize its activities in order to minimize exceptional situations (Perrow 1967).

Among the many factors that are important in setting up systems, especially in the primary operating core of an organization, are workflow uncertainty and task uncertainty, as noted in Chapter 3. Workflow uncertainty has to do with knowing when the raw material, client, or customer will enter into the operations. Task uncertainty has to do with knowledge or a lack of knowledge about how to perform the work activities. Organizations can reduce task and workflow uncertainties by instituting various buffering mechanisms. For example, the organization, particularly a manufacturing one, can stock up on inventories to protect its operations from disruptions when such inventories are difficult to secure. It may also routinize its activities and prepare employees to perform these activities in order to facilitate the smooth functioning of the operations. Using such buffering mechanisms, the organization seals off its technical core from uncertainties and in so doing treats technology as focal to its operations. Thus, technology emerges as a major, if not the major, determinant of structure at the primary operating core of manufacturing organizations, and structure assists in the protection of the technologies within the operating core. But all work organizations are not uniquely determined by the technical system. There are other alternatives.

THE EFFECTS OF THE SERVICE
ENCOUNTER ON STRUCTURE

We defined a service as an event, a deed, or a performance rendered by one person for another. To a significant degree, the output of service organizations is achieved through relationships between persons as contrasted with relationships between people and things in manufacturing organizations (Bell 1973). In service organizations, then, especially in high-contact service organizations, a transaction between the service employee and the client/customer is necessary in order to provide the service. Inherent within the transaction is the technology used in the production of such services. Clients and customers cannot be readily separated from the vital information input or raw materials they provide to the service operation and technology. Consequently, the technology is difficult to isolate from such encounters. Indeed, as noted in Chapter 3, within the encounter between the service employee and client/customer, what is being contracted upon by the client/customer and what is being delivered or sold by the service provider is the technology. The technology is the output or service.

Thus, in the operations of services the technology cannot be easily separated from the service output. And the tendency of organizations to reduce independent actions by their participants in order to minimize exceptional situations, as one would encounter within manufacturing organizations, is hardly meaningful within service operations in which clients/customers are actively involved.

Since the technology of service operations is closely lodged in the encounter and cannot be readily separated from the output generated from such encounters, the internal governance is not uniquely determined by the technical system. Instead of focusing only on technology as the primary determinant of structure in service organizations, it is necessary to examine the encounter between the service employee and the client/customer, which forms a part of the technology.

Clearly, clients and customers are important environmental elements for service organizations because they provide crucial raw material for the service operations and they interact in those activities that directly contribute to the import, conversion, and export processes. Client/customer involvement in the operating activities of services brings a segment of the external environment directly into the organization. The extent to which the operation of the organization is dependent on this segment will reflect the nature of the encounter. Consequently, the kinds of encounter will determine the internal governance or structure for service operations.

TESTING THE EFFECTS OF THE ENCOUNTER

We attempted to test the effects of the encounter on the structure of service organizations in a study of forty-one service organizations in both the United States and Sweden. These organizations were selected according to the type of encounter they had with clients and customers. Two types of service organizations were examined: maintenance-interactive and task-interactive services. For the maintenance-interactive services, banks, insurance firms, and wholesale and

Table 4-1. Breakdown of Firms by Encounter and Size.

	Size		
Nature of Encounter	Small	Large	Range in Size
Maintenance interactive	14	13	20-12,921
Task interactive	10	4	20-1,024

Table 4-2. Service Encounter According to the Approximate Time of Each Contact Episode between Employee and Client/Customer.

	Maintenance Interactive		Task Interactive
Approximate Time in Each Contact Episode	(Insurance and Banks)	(Wholesale and Retail)	(Marketing-Advertising, Engineering and Financial Consulting)
Median	5.7 min	11 min	2 hours
Mean	9.5 min	13 min	2.6 hours
Range	2 to 60 min	5 min to 3 hours	15 min to 8 hours

retail organizations were examined. For the task-interactive service encounter, marketing, advertising, engineering consulting, finance, and real estate organizations were investigated. The size dimension for the selection of these organizations was based on the number of full-time equivalent employees working at the organization. Since approximately 70 percent of all workers engaged in service activities are in organizations of less than 100 people, we used 100 as the cutoff between large and small organizations. Table 4-1 shows the breakdown of firms studied.

Data were collected through extensive interviews with at least one upper-level manager in each organization. In some instances, as many as four people were interviewed. Approximately half of those interviewed in this study were chief executive officers (CEOs). The time spent in each organization ranged from one hour and forty minutes to five hours, a median time being approximately two hours and twenty minutes. Data was gathered from top-level managers based on the notion that they would be in an advantageous position to give the specific kinds of structural configuration data that were being sought.

First, managers were asked to estimate the amount of time those employees who had direct contact with clients and customers actually spent in each encounter episode. The results are presented in Table 4-2.

THE STRUCTURAL CONFIGURATION
OF SERVICES: THE SPAN OF CONTROL

We noted earlier that one of the dimensions of structure is its configuration, or the shape and form of the organization. This dimension can highlight structural differences. One element of structural configuration examined was the span of control or direct reports in the sample of service organizations.

The notion of span of control or the number of subordinates directly responding to someone in a superior position is one of management's oldest concerns. For centuries, managers have been trying to determine the optimum number of subordinates one can effectively supervise. It is generally believed that as technology or task activities increase in complexity there is a need for more direct scrutiny of subordinates' activities. The increased difficulty of preplanning and establishing standards requires more monitoring and advising of subordinates. Consequently, closer supervision will be required, which limits the number of subordinates a manager can effectively assist or control.

There is strong support for an inverse relationship between spans of control and task complexity in manufacturing organizations. Perhaps the most comprehensive studies conducted on spans of control were undertaken by Joan Woodward (1965) and William Zwerman (1970). These researchers found that as technological complexity increased there was a corresponding decrease in the span of control (see Table 4-3).

A comprehensive analysis of spans of control in services has not been published. The few studies that have been undertaken have been very limited and have produced mixed or inconclusive results. Bell (1965) studied thirty-three departments in a general hospital and found that technological complexity and span of control tended to have an inverse relationship. Conversely, Ouchi and Dowling

Table 4-3. Median Span of Control in Manufacturing Organizations.

Production	Woodward Study	Zwerman Study
Unit or small batch production (job shop)	23	12
Mass production (assembly line)	16	10.5
Process production (chemical industrial process)	8	5

Table 4-4. Span of Control in Service Organizations.

Span of Control	Type of Encounter	
	Maintenance Interactive	Task Interactive
Median	9.5	10
Mean	10.3	9.5
Range	4-24	5-19
Most Successful Firm[a]	11	13

a. The most successful organization was determined by asking executives to rate the best-managed competitors in their industry.

(1975) studied the retail department stores and found no support for a relationship between technology and span of control.

Our approach to the determination of the span of control in the service organizations studied is consistent with that taken by earlier studies. Span of control was measured by simply dividing the number of subordinates by the number of people in supervisory positions. The median span of control for task-interactive service organizations was ten employees, slightly larger than that of maintenance-interactive service organizations. A comparison of the results found in this service organization study (Table 4-4) with those obtained from manufacturing organizations (Table 4-3) yields some interesting notions. In the manufacturing organizations observed by Joan Woodward, the median supervisory span of control for unit batch or "job shop" production was twenty-three; for mass production (assembly line) it was sixteen, and for process or continuous production it was eight. Zwerman's manufacturing study found similar results. The singular point these manufacturing studies put forth is that as task activities or technology in the operations of manufacturing organizations increases in sophistication, the number of subordinates a supervisor manages correspondingly decreases. This is sensible because as task activities become more varied and complex, supervisors will have less time to assist subordinates, and the span of control will tend to decrease. Technology is thus influencing the way these manufacturing organizations perform.

Examining the results of the service organizations, we find very little change in the relationship between the kinds of encounter and the span of control of supervisors. Although we did not examine technology directly, it can be assumed that the task activities required for task-interactive service encounters (engineering consulting) are more complex than those required in maintenance-interactive service encounters (banks and retail). Since changes in encounter did not significantly change the span of supervisory control, it can also be inferred that changes in technology would have no significant effect on the span of control.

It is surprising that a more pronounced association did not appear between the nature of the encounter and the number of employees a supervisor can manage in service organizations. One would have expected a relatively larger span of control in low-encounter service organizations (retail, banks) because it is generally believed that the nature of what people in these organizations actually do when they interact with customers lends itself more readily to the introduction of systems. But we have found that the span of control dimension of structure, especially at the primary operating core, varied only slightly across service organizations.

The data show that there are smaller spans of control in the service organizations studied than in the manufacturing organizations of earlier works. This difference is partially due to the nature of the operations between manufacturing and services. In manufacturing operations it is possible to protect the conversion subsystem of the transformation system by various buffering mechanisms (e.g., stocking up on inventory, preparing employees). By reducing uncertainty, the organization can preplan and establish systems. Consequently, a separation can be made in the decisionmaking process between decision control and decision management. At the lower levels, decision management will be in force where employees, especially at the primary operating core, are engaged in some initiating of ideas, activities, and suggestions, but more likely in implementing activities already ratified. Further, it is at the higher levels that we can expect to find the decision control where there is ratification and inspection of the decision being implemented at the lower levels.

The ability to separate the decisionmaking process and have only the decision management at the lower levels effectively reduces the number of activities and also the complexity of the activity an employee will perform. Standardization of these activities can be established with indirect supervision because the employee is partially supervised by the preplanned operations. Thus, a supervisor can monitor a larger number of subordinates at the workflow because the supervisor is being aided by standardized operations, and errors can be easily detected and corrective actions taken.

The span of control in services is more problematic. Service organizations are fundamentally information-processing entities, information forming the basic raw material in their operations. This is so irrespective of the nature of the interaction or encounter with clients or customers. Both low-encounter and high-encounter service organizations must secure information raw material from clients/customers in order to complete the service output. The direct encounter between the service provider and client/customer requires varying degrees of skills in activities surrounding the soliciting of needed information, the processing of information, and the delivery or dissemination of information output to the client/customer. Each of these activities is complex because it emerges from reactive and potentially uncertain exchanges with clients/customers. Take, for example, the simplest set of activities involved in the delivery of the service to clients/customers in, say, the encounter between a sales clerk and the customer in a retail store. Even here, the notion of courtesy—making the customer feel welcome in the exchange or operation—can be idiosyncratic. The smile or other pleasantries, verbal or nonverbal exchange acceptable to one customer may not be acceptable to another. Such activities are difficult to specify and control. Thus, the direct encounter between the service provider and the client or customer, irrespective of the activity—be it securing information, processing the information, or delivering services—requires relatively complex skills. Further, in order to complete their task activities, contact employees are required to possess skills for the inspection and correction of errors and for control. These are inherent task activities present in all service encounters.

Given the nature of service encounters, it is more difficult for the organization to separate the decisionmaking process into decision management and decision control. Service providers in these encounters must be allowed some autonomy to engage in decision management, that is, initiating and implementing solutions in the face of client/customer reaction to novel situations, and some control over these decisions (deciding which actions to take along with monitoring these actions so that necessary corrections can be made). Given this kind of autonomy there is a potential for the service employee to be opportunistic. The supervisor, but more often, the employee may simply be in need of assistance. For these reasons direct supervision is required in the service operations, irrespective of the nature of the encounter. Only a limited number of employees can be effectively managed in direct supervision—hence the relatively smaller number of employees found in the service organizations studied.

THE CHIEF EXECUTIVE SPAN OF CONTROL

Another structural configuration of organizations is the span of control of the chief executive officer. The CEO is actually the top manager or the managing director of the organization, and his or her raw span of control is determined by the number of employees directly responding to him or her.

It is generally believed that the number of people a CEO of a manufacturing organization can effectively supervise is dependent on the degree of technological complexity. Studies have tended to support this proposition. Both Woodward and Zwerman in their extensive studies showed such an association. Table 4–5 shows the results of these studies, which found that as the complexity of the technology increases the number of people responding to the CEO increases.

In the service organizations studied a different pattern emerged. Table 4–6 shows the number of people responding to the CEO decreasing as the complexity of the encounter with clients or customers increases. CEOs of maintenance-interactive service organizations were found to have a median score of 6.5 employees with a range of 2 to 20 employees. Their counterparts in the task-interactive service organizations were found to have a median score of 4.5 employees and a range of 2 to 7 employees.

Table 4-5. Span of Control of Chief Executive Officers in Manufacturing Organizations.

Type of Manufacturing Technology	Woodward's Study		Zwerman's Study	
	Median	Range	Median	Range
Unit and small batch production (job shop)	4	2-9	5	1-9
Mass production (assembly line)	7	4-13	6	3-15
Process production (chemical industry)	10	5-19	5.5	4-14

Table 4-6. Span of Control of Chief Executive Officers in Service Organizations.

Span of Control	Service Encounter	
	Maintenance Interactive	Task Interactive
Median	6.5	4.5
Mean	7.4	4.3
Range	2-20	2-7

One explanation for the difference between manufacturing and service sector organizations may lie in how these organizations are structured. As the technology within the operating core of manufacturing organizations becomes complex, there is a tendency to buffer such operations from outside disturbances. The object is to create an environment in which the system can operate with as little interruption as possible so that optimum efficiency can be realized. It is primarily to this end that these operations will be closed off or perform as if they were closed systems. In order to protect the core, rules, guidelines, and regulations have to be established throughout the organization. There is a separation of the decisionmaking process within these organizations with decision management (initiation and implementation) at the lower levels and decision control (ratification and inspection) at the higher levels. However, guidelines will still be pervasive throughout the organizations. Although such guidelines will be relatively fewer at the top, there is still some dependence on them at this level. The presence of rules and regulations suggests that some predictability of people's behavior can be maintained. Consequently, less direct supervision will be required of the CEO as guidelines can be established for subordinates. This makes it possible to increase the number of people responding to the CEO as one moves from the less complex operation (unit production) to the more complex operations (process production) (see Table 4–5).

Conversely, the chief executive span of control in the service context is based on another rationale. Richard Daft's (1978) notion of "dual cores" is most applicable to the service context. There are two core technologies in services—one at the operations level and another at the administrative level. Within the primary operating core the service provider is involved with pivotal (main or primary service exchanges) encounters with clients/customers. At the administrative level the service provider is either protected from client/customer interaction or is engaged in relevant encounters (supplemental to the service) with clients/customers.

Invariably, services executives are more directly engaged in administrative activities in supervising and coordinating the heads of functional units. Since the administrative activities are generally buffered from much client/customer involvement, less uncertainty surrounds these activities. It is thus possible to predict and plan for the administrative activities and in so doing establish systems.

Within the administrative arena, the CEO can separate the decision-making process by delegating decision management to his or her direct reports while maintaining decision control. In such a separation, guidelines, rules, and regulations can be established in order to assist the chief executive decision control activities.

The degree to which the administrative arena can be segmented into decision control and decision management is a function of what occurs in the primary operating core. When the pivotal encounters are of a relatively low level (e.g., retail organizations) then more rules and regulations can be developed for the activities and the greater will be the separation between the administrative arena and the primary operating core. Conversely, when the pivotal encounter in the primary operating core is high or complex, the fewer will be the rules and regulations, and the separation between decision management and control will not be very pronounced. In other words, there will be less of a dual core within the organization.

When the decisionmaking process can be separated within the administration core, the CEO can supervise a relatively larger number of direct reports because the established rules and regulations can assist the individual in regulating behavior. On the other hand, when it is difficult to separate the decisionmaking process into decision management and decision control, the chief executive will supervise relatively fewer direct reports. In the absence of rules and regulations to guide the behavior of people, direct supervision or more personal assistance will be required. It is for these reasons that we find the CEO's span of control larger for maintenance-interactive services than for task-interactive services, as Table 4–6 shows. In the task-interactive organizations the dual core is less pronounced than in the maintenance-interactive services. Thus, there is a decrease in the number of direct reports to the chief executive as the service encounter with clients and customers become more complex.

LEVELS OF MANAGEMENT

A structural configuration variable that is closely tied to the span of control in organizations is the number of levels of authority within the hierarchy. This aspect of structure can be determined by measuring the number of levels of supervision or management between the primary operating core beginning with the first line supervisor up to and including the CEO. The number of levels of management largely reflects the authority structure because it indicates who has the right to make certain decisions.

Joan Woodward found that in manufacturing organizations there is a direct link between technological complexity and the number of levels of management. This was later corroborated by the work of Zwerman. These researchers found that as the complexity of the technology in the core operations increased, there was a corresponding increase in the number of levels of management, as Table 4–7 shows. This may be due to the number of support systems that are necessary to protect such technology.

For the service organizations examined in this investigation, a different pattern from that observed in the manufacturing sectors was

Table 4–7. Managerial Levels in Manufacturing Organizations.

Type of Manufacture Technology	Median Levels of Management	
	Woodward's Study	Zwerman's Study
Unit or small batch production	3	4
Mass production	4	5
Process production	6	6

Table 4–8. Levels of Management for Service Organizations.

Number of Levels of Management	Types of Service Encounter	
	Maintenance Interactive	Task Interactive
Median	4	3
Mean	3	2
Range	2–5	2–3
Most Successful Firm[a]	4	2

a. The most successful organization was determined by asking executives to rate the best-managed competitors in their industry.

found. Within these service organizations the number of levels of management was found to be inversely related to the complexity of the encounter between the service employee and the client or customer.

Table 4–8 shows fewer levels of management for these service organizations than that found in earlier manufacture studies. The table also shows that the high or more complex encounter organizations have a slightly lower number of management levels than less complex encounter service organizations. The relative flatness of these organizations is largely attributable to the autonomy and authority that must be given to the worker in the service operations so that the worker can address the uncertainty created by the clients'/ customers' presence in the operations. For these service providers there will be less of a separation in the decisionmaking process, as both decision management and decision control will be in the domain of the service provider in these encounters.

The relative flatness of the services serves a useful purpose for the decisionmaking process within these organizations: Porter and Lawler (1968) have observed that "decision risk" increases as the number of levels of management increases. The primary reason for this increase is the lapse in time that occurs between the implementation of a decision and the point when feedback on the effects of that decision is received. Organizations operating in stable environments (e.g., manufacturing organizations) will tend to be vertically decentralized with many levels of management and more tolerance for the uncertainty created by a delay in information transmitted to the actual decisionmaker. Conversely, service operations that are in dynamic and unstable environments will need to respond to relatively uncertain situations directly created by the client's/customer's involvement in the operations. Because there is less tolerance for decision risks in these organizations, there are fewer levels of management.

SIZE AND THE DESIGN OF SERVICE ORGANIZATIONS

It is widely believed that the design of an organization is affected by the size of the organization—that as organizations increase in size there would be a corresponding increase in structural complexity. This means that as the number of people in an organization increases there is a tendency to specialize the task activities, standardize many of the components, and increase the levels of management in order to reduce the loss of control. One would reasonably expect that smaller organizations would tend to have a smaller number of their employees involved in, for example, administrative functions than would a larger organization.

Much of the empirical support for these assumptions has emerged from manufacturing sector organizations. The relationship is less clear for the service organizations studied. Table 4-9 shows the association between size and a number of structural components for service organizations. It is readily apparent that the structural components show some interesting associations with size.

The number of levels of management changed only slightly with size. Generally, an increase in management levels indicates that the administration is becoming elaborate. There is a tendency for the

Table 4-9. The Relationship between Size and Structural Factors in Service Organizations.[a]

| | Number of Employees | | | | | |
| | 100 or less | | 101–499 | | 500 or more | |
Configuration Factors	Median	Range	Median	Range	Median	Range
Levels of management	2	2-3	3	2-4	4	3-5
Chief executive						
Span of control	5	2-15	6	2-9	4	2-20
Span of first						
Line supervisor	12	4-19	14	8-15	14	6-24

a. Size = number of full-time equivalent employees.

organization to make a distinction between the primary operating core activities and the activities for governing within the core. Consequently, formalization increases as rules, regulations, and procedures are established to cope with the addition of new employees without losing control. But in the service organizations studied such formalization of activities does not appear to occur. Although the levels of management seem to increase slightly with size, Table 4-9 also shows that the span of control of the first line supervisor hardly changes with size.

If formality increases with size then one would expect this to be reflected in the number of people the first line manager can effectively supervise or control. As rules and procedures are established there is less of a need for direct or personal supervision, and consequently a manager can regulate a larger number of subordinates. But the relationship between size and span of control may be curvilinear. Large spans of management control may occur in uncertain environments where activities cannot be regulated by rules and procedures. In such situations, which call for novel techniques in the face of novel problems, employees have to be given broad guidelines and use discretion so that they can perform in an appropriate way. Decision management and decision control will be controlled by the service provider. With such autonomy it is unnecessary to supervise closely these employees because the supervisor will generally not be in possession of any more specific knowledge about issues that are idiosyncratic than is the subordinate in the encounter, especially when such encounters are high in uncertainty or complexity. This makes it possible for a manager's span to increase.

The presence of clients and customers in service operations can create uncertainty for the organization, as earlier noted. When the potential for such uncertainty exists, there is a tendency toward less formalization of activities by rules and procedures. Since our service data show no meaningful change as one moves across the various size categories, there may be some support for Child and Manfield's observation that for service organizations there is a tendency toward relatively unbureaucratic forms or less formalization at all sizes.

THE MODERATING EFFECTS OF CUSTOMER-FIRM INTERFACE

It seems clear that technology is important in the design of service organizations. But it does not appear that the relationship is simple and direct, as found in manufacturing organizations. The client/customer involvement in the operations of services will tend to affect the relationship between technology and structure. Indeed, the relationship between technology and structure will be moderated by the direct face-to-face interaction between the service provider and the client/customer. The technology is the service that is contracted for by clients and customers, and the nature of such technology or service will be reflected by the nature of the contract. But the activities within service exchanges entail more than just the service being provided to the client/customer. As a contract between the service provider and the client/customer, the encounter will involve potential activities such as negotiation of contracts between the client/customer, production and delivery of the service, monitoring to ensure that opportunism is controlled, and bonding. Consequently, the extent to which technology is related to or determines the structure of the service organizations is contractually moderated. When there is specific or low contact between the service provider and the client/customer, there is relatively less dependence on face-to-face contact, and technology will have a greater impact on structure. This is because as clients'/customers' involvement in the operating activities decreases there is a corresponding reduction in uncertainty. Consequently, it is possible to seal off the technical core within the context of a closed system logic that entails assumptions of cause-effect relations. But when the contract between the service provider and client/customer is uncertain, nonspecific, or complex, technology will have less of an impact on structure. Such service operations do not lend themselves to closed system assumptions. It may be that moving toward closed systems logic in the conversion process is counterproductive because it would tend to inhibit the reciprocal exchanges and the mutual adjustment between the client/customer and the individual service employee. In order for service employees to perform their task activities in a relatively uncertain open system capacity, buffers will have to be decreased. One would expect a decentralization of the decisionmaking process. Centralization of the decision management in the presence of increasing client/customer involvement would cause the unit to be overwhelmed with information. Since decision control and decision management will not easily be separated at the operations level, service providers as independent decision units will have to be afforded the discretion to influence kinds of transformations and establish the appropriate structural framework for the production of the service. It is possible, therefore, "for lower-level decision makers to implement structures more consistent with their structural preferences and motivational orientations" (Bobbitt and Ford 1980: 70). For these service operations, structure will be more related to the customer-firm face-to-face contact, as there will be more dependence on the client's/customer's direct personal contributions in the production process. We would therefore expect that services with comparatively low customer inclusion and with low dependency on the lower client/customer-employee interface (e.g., bank tellers, retail clerks) would have less individual employee involvement with clients/customers than services with high dependency on customer-employee interface (e.g., nurses, physicians, consultants). Since the client/customer involvement directly affects the service provider's task activities, variations in the dependency on customer-employee face-to-face contact would be expected to generate variations in the relationship between technology and structure at the service operations (see Figure 4-1).

In sum, the client/customer is an integral part of the service operating activities because he or she provides information that is essential for the input, conversion, and export processes. Clients/customers constitute a significant contingency at the service operations and therefore one that is not amenable to a closed system logic. Access to

Figure 4-1. Centrality of the Customer-Firm Interface Variable in Service Organizations.

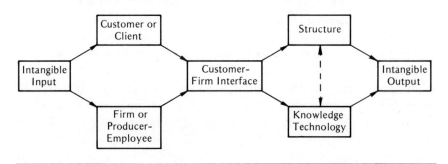

crucial information makes it counterproductive to centralize structures. Moreover, the variable nature of the raw material (information) provided by the client/customer impacts upon any functional relationship between the service provider's technology and structure around the operations. In other words, the technology-structure relationship may not be constant across variations of unit transactions concerning the extent to which the client/customer is incorporated into the service production process of the service employee. Hence, the client/customer can be thought of as a "moderator" variable with respect to the functional unit structure of technology-structure relationships. It would seem reasonable that the extent to which the service organization is dependent on the client's/customer's direct input affects how much that organization can control and allocate its resources in a cost-effective way.

SUMMARY

In the structuring of service activities two important properties to consider are technology and the client-employee interaction. Technology is directly related to structure in low-contact service operations. Within the operations of these organizations clients'/customers' involvement is relatively limited. As a result, transformation activities can be readily sealed off and subjected to job rationalization. In this context, clients/customers can be decoupled from the production process and predictability can be obtained by a streaming of customer flow and automation (e.g., ATMs).

The direct influence of technology on structure in high-contact services is relatively less pronounced. Clients/customers are active participants in the operations of these organizations. The customer-firm interaction is a moderator in the relationship between technology and structure and reflects the service demands, complexity, and client/customer involvement. As this interaction increases in complexity, the structure of the organization has to be extended to allow for an active client/customer participation in production activities.

Structures that would invite the employee's direct involvement with the client/customer should be consistent with the separation of decision management and control. This is because in the face of high task and workflow uncertainty, and where there is little job interdependence, entrepreneurial self-control will engender more effective use of the organization's resources. This would further imply that the structure of the organization would have to adjust to afford the service provider in direct contact with the client/customer the opportunity to absorb many traditional management activities (e.g., determining work methods, control of resources, and interfacing with clients/customers).

The view of the customer-firm interface as a moderator in the relationship between technology and structure is useful. As a moderator variable, the client/customer involvement improves our prediction by identifying the organizations for which technology as a predictor of structure is more valid.

5 THE QUALITATIVE SIDE OF STRUCTURE IN SERVICES

The discussion in Chapter 4 centered around an objective perspective of structure in service organizations. Structure was viewed as the enduring traits of an organization that are reflected in how the positions are distributed and related to one another (James and Jones 1976). Some dimensions of this view of structure are the division of labor, size of work groups, configuration, and spans of control. The objectivity associated with this view arises from the fact that one can actually observe or directly apprehend these dimensions. The objective view is an effort to regulate possible lines of action about the observable world within the organization (Simon 1957).

The adequacy of objective structures in completely controlling the behavior of people in service organizations is highly questionable. This is because, as Kolodny (1979) notes, after members of the organization have learned the kinds of behaviors that are required of their positions and the relationships of such positions to others, objective structural control mechanisms become relatively redundant.

Objective structures are less influential as the uncertainty surrounding task activities increases. One would therefore expect the effects of objective structure to decrease as the involvement of clients/customers in service operations increases. This chapter will examine the subjective side of structure, which is also of immense importance as a control mechanism within services.

VALUE-SUBJECTIVE STRUCTURES

The general structure of service organizations was earlier conceptualized as the ways the firm divides up the work it has to accomplish and how these work activities are coordinated. Thus, the structure of any service firm is simply a set of relationships among its members. Information is the raw material that service employees gather and process. Clients/customers are allowed into the production process of the organization both in order to provide efficiently such information and to be better consumers of the output generated from such involvement. This is crucial to the actual decision process pertinent to the rendering of services to clients/customers. The service provider must first secure the raw information from clients/customers or in some cases other employees; then, after such information is processed, a decision is made on the best way to provide the service.

There is always a framework around the decisionmaking process that dictates the kinds of decisions that are made and the effectiveness with which the service is rendered to clients/customers. Each step in the decisionmaking process entails two fundamental aspects. George Simmel (1908) refers to these as the "form" and "content" of structure. Simmel's breakdown closely resembles Herbert Simon's (1957) framework of "value" and "factual" elements of structure. The contents or facts of a situation are those elements that are without structure and are determined in themselves. In other words, contents are the "objects" in a situation, such as the raw information received from the client/customer. Forms, on the other hand, are the synthesizing aspects of a situation that exist primarily to select objects from basic experience and combine them into determinate units. In other words, the form serves to make sense of the often varied kinds of information that are actually gathered.

When the service provider makes a decision regarding the kind of service to render to clients/customers, two complex sets of judgments are required. One set concerns the facts that are relevant to the situation; the other has to do with the significance of these facts and how they are interpreted. Although both of these elements influence the service provider's behavior, the decisionmaking process has to begin with some value structure that is taken as a given (Simon 1957).

One of the central purposes of value structures within organizations is to give consistency to behavior. Without values the behavior of people within organizations would be reduced to merely reacting to stimuli (Kluckholn 1952). It is not the objective constraints of structure, such as rules and regulations, that cause action but rather the organization members' values to adhere to the norms or rules where these exist. Consequently, the organization can secure some degree of predictability over the behavior of its members through the value system. To a large extent, then, values serve both to discriminate among possible courses of action and to rationalize individual behavior or actions that are taken (Stymne 1970).

THE RATIONALITY OF SUBJECTIVE STRUCTURES

It seems clear that the selection of events by people from their experiences within organizations must be preceded by an interpretation of such factors. The structure that surrounds the selection and interpretation of events is confined by what Simmel calls the "subjective intention" of the person. In other words, people involved in the processing of information in service organizations must first interpret such information within the context of motives, purposes, and intentions.

It should be made clear at this point that the notion of motive or intention does not refer to the psychological states of people within organizations. We are not concerned here with the service provider's status of "feelings." Instead, we are addressing what Max Weber refers to as rational interpretation, the notion that the motives behind the employee's interpretation are based on subjective meanings that appear to that person to be adequate grounds for the conduct. Thus, the organization member's behavior is constrained by "value-rational" structures to which there is conscious adherence (Weber 1968).

Subjective intention is very important, especially for the service provider in organizations where much uncertainty surrounds the task activities and where it is difficult to establish complete contracts with clients/customers—for example, the pivotal exchanges in health care or legal consulting. For the service employees in these encounters, activities cannot be governed solely by objective structural dimensions such as rules, regulations, procedures, and so on. Instead, these service providers must depend largely on value-rational structures, which are in turn dictated by the "situational logic" (Popper 1962).

The notion of a subjective or value-rational structure entails an organization structure that is quite distinct from the "objective" structure. The subjective structure is a type of authority based on the organization member's confidence in an absolute value of a rationalized set of norms (Willers 1967; Weber 1968). Subjective structure centers around the intention of the individual and serves as a framework not only for the interpretation of input, but also as a basis for discriminating among possible courses of action. Consequently, the service organization can secure compliance from its members through adherence to ideological norms and to formal rules and regulations of objective structures. In sum then, members of service organizations function simultaneously with two types of structures: an objective structure and a value-rational structure.

AN EMPIRICAL STUDY OF THE EFFECTS OF SUBJECTIVE STRUCTURES

There is much empirical data to support the hypothesis that technology is related to objective structure in organizations. The implication here is that the technology within the primary operating core will determine the kinds of structure necessary to govern activities around the operations. Very little attention has been directed to the subjective side of structure in organizations and its relationship to other important organization properties such as technology and objective structure.

Since technology and objective structure are salient properties in the functioning of service organizations, we will examine empirically the effects of the subjective structure on these elements. We have defined technology as all of the activities employed in the conversion of an input into an output with or without the use of machines. It was also indicated earlier that objective structure involves an authority structure consisting of rules, regulations, procedures, and so on. From these perspectives, both technology and objective structure are "factual" elements. These organization properties are elements of a situation whose meaning must be determined by members. The effects of technology on service organization structure will be affected by the subjective structure.

Members of service organizations are to a great extent engaged in the processing of information in their attempts to render a service to clients/customers. Some of this information raw material is obtained from other service workers, but most comes directly from clients/customers. Many years ago Chester Barnard (1938) pointed out the association between communication or information-processing patterns and the objective structure within organizations. This link is based on the authority structure. Since value structures cannot be separated from the process of communication (Gellerman 1968), one might reasonably expect the service provider's value structures to be related to perceived objective structures.

In the interaction between service providers and clients/customers there is a degree of uncertainty inherent in the encounter and accordingly a degree of uncertainty around the kinds of services that are contracted upon. This would suggest that there may be several possible ways to go about completing the task activities. If technology involves a knowledge of the ways to accomplish task activities, then the actual decisions made by the service provider in providing the service can be construed as technology.

The fact that the service provider has to make a decision regarding the kinds of activities necessary to provide the service suggests that alternatives are at his or her disposal. Such alternatives are factual elements subject to the interpretation of the service provider in deciding on a course of action. And values form the basis for comparing possible courses of action. Furthermore, the correctness of the service provider's decision is meaningful only within the context of subjective values (Simon 1957).

In comparing services and manufacturing organizations, we would reasonably expect to find that the subjective structure of employees relates more directly to objective structure in service organizations than in manufacturing organizations. Since a service is a deed or an effort, service organizations characteristically produce an intangible output. This contrasts with the tangible output of manufacturing. Further, service organizations tend to be highly dependent on an intricate personal interface between the service provider and clients/customers. The production process in services is not restricted to the confines of the employee's work domain; rather, the conventional environmental boundaries are extended significantly in order to involve the client/customer actively as an indispensable part of the output function. This sharply contrasts with the work situation of manufacturing organizations, in which employees at the primary operating core are usually buffered from the external environment.

The inclusion of clients/customers in the production process creates relatively more uncertainty for service employees than for manufacturing at the primary operating core. Since the presence of uncertainty in task activities suggests that there may be many possible ways of addressing an issue, one would expect subjective structures to be more pronounced and have a larger impact on the functioning of service operations than on manufacturing operations.

TESTING OUR PROPOSITION

Two sets of data were collected for our research. One source of data, as outlined in Chapter 4, was obtained from thirty-eight service organizations from the private sector. Since our hypotheses are directed at the operations level of organizations, we attempted to isolate the workflow, defined by Bakke (1959) as the production and distribution of output, within each firm. One simple but practical way of teasing out an organization's workflow is to examine the task activities that engage the largest number of employees, as Pugh, Hickson and associates (1969) have done. Since a fundamental characteristic of service operations is direct personal interface between the producer and the consumer of the service, only employees having direct contact with clients/customers (and in pivotal encounters) were selected for participation in this investigation. Within each service organization questionnaires were distributed to employees, and 620 usable questionnaires were collected for a 49 percent response rate. All responses were voluntary and anonymous.

The second part of the study was conducted in two manufacturing organizations. An assembly-line-like operation best depicts the nature of the workflow operation within these organizations. Both organizations mass produced their outputs. Questionnaires were administered on-site to groups of employees (in a nonsupervisory capacity), and data were gathered from different shifts on the assembly lines. Responses were voluntary and anonymous. Of the full-time employees in these organizations, 109 usable questionnaires were obtained for a response rate of 74 percent.

MEASUREMENT OF THE VARIABLES

Heavy emphasis was placed on employing measures that have been used in earlier studies in order to maintain consistency with these efforts. Standard scores were computed for all variables in the present investigation. (See Appendix 5A for a detailed discussion of the instruments used, the analysis of the data, and the presentation of the results.)

THE IMPLICATIONS OF THE RESULTS

The findings in this study provide some support for the general proposition that work values mediate the relationship between an organization's objective structure and technology. Specifically, the findings show that the service provider's work values relate significantly to perceived objective structure.

The data also indicate that the objective structure-work values relationship is somewhat more pronounced in the service organization than in the manufacturing organization. This may be due, in part, to the largely discretionary characteristic of service task activities, especially as they pertain to the direct interaction with the client/customer. This situation "requires" the service employee to form judgments as to the probability that particular actions will lead to some desired end when providing the service to clients/customers. Consequently, as Simon (1957) notes, the "correctness" of the decisions made by the service provider may have meaning and guidance only in terms of the subjective work values held by the individual. Conversely, within the manufacturing context, it may be that the rational premise to which the technology generally lends itself reduces the employee's discretion and the range of decisionmaking. Thus, one would tend to expect less reliance on intrinsic work values as a means of controlling behavior.

EXPANDING THE TECHNOLOGY-STRUCTURE PARADIGM

The purpose of our research was to test the effects of subjective structures on the relationship between technology and objective structure in service organizations. The empirical results from this study should be treated with caution due to the inherent limitations of the research. First, none of the constructs was actually observed. Instead, the findings were primarily based on perceptual data. Further, although an attempt was made to conceptually create independent measures of intrinsic and convenience work value structures, the correlation between them was significant.

Within these limitations, the data imply a more expansive perspective on the structuring of service organizations. Conventionally, as pointed out earlier, there is widespread support for the paradigm that a close relationship exists between the technology of an organization and its objective structure. Drawing heavily on the work of Thompson (1967), we viewed organizations as averse to uncertainty. Under norms of rationality, organizations will strive to seal off their core technologies from environmental influences. Thus, in order to capitalize on their determinate nature, organizations seek to adjust their technical core structure to the demands of their technological core. This allows for efficient coordination and scheduling of interdependent parts.

The results of the current study suggest that value structures are important links between organizational technology and objective structure. This finding is consistent with Simon's observation that to consider structural activity as "valuationally neutral is an abstraction from reality" (1957: 184). Accordingly, the two types of structure investigated in this study—individual work value or subjective structure and objective structure—present two modes of securing consistency of behavior of organization participants. Organizations will attempt to guide the decisions made by their participants through these structural mechanisms. Since the decisionmaking process, according to Simon (1957), must begin with some value premise (generally taken as a given), value or subjective structures serve as the means that connect the technical activities with the objective structural end. Accordingly, the individual subjective system serves as an important link between objective structure and technology, mediating, in fact, the relationship between these two variables.

The current study sought to expand the conventional view of organization structure by dividing this construct into its subjective (values) and object perspectives. It is therefore possible, as the findings indicate, to establish new relationships with technology in service organizations and to move toward a preliminary addition to the technology-structure paradigm.

APPLICATION TO SERVICES

One could speculate as to possible alternative interpretations of the findings of this study as they relate to service organizations. Such interpretation, however, should be treated with caution in light of the absence of comparable manufacturing organizations and the perceptual nature of the data. Given these limits, the findings do provide some clues into the practices of service organizations.

A germane characteristic of service operations is the dependence they place on the client/customer both to provide the information that constitutes the raw material to be worked on and to enter into the production process. Thus, especially in high-contact services, the client/customer is directly involved in the production of his or her own wants. This arrangement builds a great deal of potential uncertainty into each contact episode because the client's/customer's behavior cannot be anticipated with any regularity. Thus further, a high degree of variability in the activities required of the service provider in response to clients/customers can be expected and will be a continuous source of ambiguity for organizational action.

This uncertainty serves to generate equivocal types of information for the service employee. For example, when a patient relays to his or her physician that he or she is experiencing a pain in the abdomen, there are many ways for the physician to interpret this symptom, as the information is equivocal. The notion of information equivocality suggests information that is of a qualitative nature (Daft and Macintosh 1981). One would expect the service provider to place considerable reliance on his or her inward structures (values) as a guide for possible insights and actions in addressing clients' problems. Kluckhohn (1952) suggests that this individual value structure resides within the larger organizational structure. Such a phenomenon may indeed account for the strong association between work values and objective structure found in our study.

Conversely, the relatively weaker correspondence between work values or subjective structures and objective structure found for the manufacturing organization may be explained in terms of technology within the organization. The potential to buffer the core operations subjects the production process to rational activities and establishes systems. There is a corresponding reduction in both the equivocality of information confronting the manufacturing employee and the discretion in the task activities since only a limited set of decisions

can be correctly made for the established systems to function efficiently. Value might, therefore, be less relevant in manufacturing
organizations than one would expect in services.

AN EXTENDED MODEL OF
TECHNOLOGY-STRUCTURE
RELATIONSHIPS FOR SERVICES

Figure 5-1 presents a model for the association between technology
and structure as it relates specifically to service organizations. The
model suggests a view of service organizations as largely information-
processing entities—a perspective that has gained increasing interest
in the literature. Consequently, information forms the raw material,
its main source being the client/customer. The crucial role played by
the client/customer in service operations has been discussed in earlier
chapters. This view is consistent with the transactional nature of service operations (Thompson 1962) in which there is an exchange and
in which contracts are established in a personal way between the service employee and the client/customer.

This model suggests that the service organization has within its
domain two potential value systems or subjective structures. One
subjective structure emanates from the service employee and the

Figure 5-1. An Extended Model of the Technology–Structure Relationship
in Service Organizations Incorporating Value or Subjective Structures.

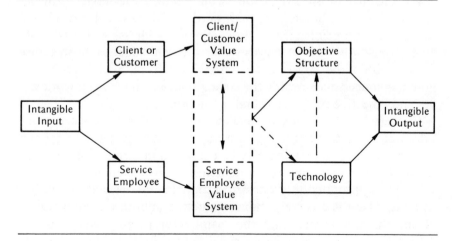

other from the client/customer. The findings in this investigation suggest that employee work values or subjective structures mediate between objective structure and technology. One could reasonably expect that the client's/customer's value system would play a similar role since their direct input into the service production is as crucial as that of the service employee.

SUMMARY

There are two fundamental structures in service organizations, an objective and a subjective one. As the necessity for clients'/customers' participation in service operations increases there is less dependence on the objective structures. The face-to-face exchanges, especially between the service provider and the client/customer, tend to generate an internal environment that is largely relational. The frequent trial-and-error techniques would seem to question the adequacy of objective structure in directing the behavior of the organization's participants. In relational environments there is a greater emphasis on the subjective side of structure. Subjective structures are inner states of the individual that serve to discriminate among possible courses of action and also serve as the rationale for individual behavior. Organizations can use the socialization process to inculcate their members with appropriate value structures. This process will be examined in Chapter 9. It seems reasonable to conclude that subjective or value structures perform a crucial role in guiding and directing the service provider's behavior when the object structure is inappropriate.

APPENDIX 5A

Subjective Value Structures

Although the notion of values has received much attention conceptually, there appears to be relatively little consensus regarding its measurement. A review by Brown (1976) suggests that existing scales are of questionable applicability to work organizations. For instance, value structure has been measured by organization climate measures (Payne and Pugh 1976; Schneider and Bartlett 1970; Litwin and

Stringer 1968). Some scales are of a global nature and attempt to apprehend the value construct from a macrosocietal perspective (Kluckholn 1952). Others are limited to specific domains (Scott 1965). Other studies, as Keller (1975) notes, have not clearly delineated between the value construct on the one hand and the constructs of traits, attitudes, and occupational interests on the other.

In order to address individual value structures in organizations it is necessary to distinguish between macrosocietal values and organizational or "work values." In making such a distinction, Kalleberg notes that work values are a special segment of the general concept of "values" and "reflect the individual's awareness of the condition he seeks from the work situation, and that regulate his actions in pursuit of that condition (1977: 129)." In other words, work values can be defined as the desirable factors people hold in their work-related activities.

Within this study an attempt is made to make a conceptual distinction between values and needs which have often been so closely linked in the literature. Locke (1969) defines needs in terms of what is required objectively for an individual's well-being. Values, on the other hand, have to do with an awareness of a desired state. Although values may or may not be associated with needs, values are responsible for an individual's behavior and emotional response. Lee (1948) summarizes the association by suggesting that values can only emerge within the context of need but are not necessarily identified with needs.

The approach adopted to the measurement of the value construct for this study draws largely from the work of Kalleberg (1977). In this study, work is viewed as having no inherent meaning. Instead, whatever meaning work might have is imputed by the organization's participants. Thus, he identifies individual work values by specifying a set of possible gratifications and then assesses the importance participants place on these factors. By factor analyzing the intercorrelations of thirty-four job characteristics, Kalleberg produces essentially two fundamental dimensions: "intrinsic" and "convenience," which were found to be differentially valued.

The intrinsic dimensions of work values entail those characteristics directly related to the task itself. Specifically, an intrinsic dimension addresses such factors as the extent to which the work is interesting, affords autonomy and self-direction. "Valuation of this discussion, thus, reflects the worker's desire to be stimulated and challenged by the job and to be able to exercise acquired skills at work" (Kalleberg 1977: 128). The convenience dimension has to do with the physical comforts afforded by the job. Some of the characteristics of this dimension are pleasant physical surroundings, financial considerations, supervision, and relationships with co-workers. This dimension is intended to reflect a valuation of factors that are considered to be external to the task itself.

Within the present study, intrinsic values were measured by four questions concerning the importance of the job factors of responsibility, challenge, achievement, and meaningful work. Participants responded to the importance of these factors on five-point Likert scales in the services sample and seven-point scales in the manufacturing setting. The coefficient alpha for the intrinsic items was 0.73 in the service sample and 0.59 in the manufacturing organization. The convenience values were represented by four items assessing the importance of the job factors of salary, status, working conditions, and supervision. Coefficient alpha was 0.64 in the service sample and 0.69 in the manufacturing sample.

Objective Structure

Following the work of other researchers (Glisson 1978; Hrebiniak 1974; Mohr 1971; Hage and Aiken 1969), we measured objective structure by the degree of centralization of the decisionmaking process. Individual responses to four Likert scale items were averaged to reflect the degree of decisionmaking dispersion in the organization, that is, structure. Three of these items were taken from Mohr (1971) and Hrebiniak (1974). The fourth item was a general statement paralleling the Hage and Aiken (1969) centralization conceptualization. One sample question was: "How much opportunity is there to participate in the supervisory decisions that affect the important aspects of your job?" In Glisson's (1978) study of human service organizations this measure of structure was significantly correlated with other structural measures (e.g., hierarchy of authority, division of labor, and procedural specifications). Dewar et al. (1980) concluded that the reliability and validity (convergent and discriminant) of the centralization measure of organization structure was very good. Coefficient alpha in this study was 0.82 in the service sample and 0.71 in the manufacturing sample.

Table 5A-1.   Standard Score Means and Standard Deviations.

	Service (N = 620)		Manufacturing (N = 109)	
	$\overline{X}$	S.D.	$\overline{X}$	S.D.
Structure	.25	1.05	.231	1.00
Task Complexity	-.45	1.16	-.050	1.03
Task Integration	-.189	1.30	-.000	1.00
Intrinsic Work Values	.286	1.05	.207	.78
Convenience Work Values	.538	.96	.290	.97

Technology

Consistent with the earlier works of other researchers, technology was operationalized along two dimensions: task (technological) complexity and task (technological) integration. Task complexity was measured by the degree of task routine (Mohr 1971; Glisson 1978): "To what extent do you perform the same operation over and over again?" Task integration was measured by the degree of task interdependence (Mohr 1971; Hrebiniak 1974). "To what extent do the tasks you perform require you to check with or collaborate with others?" These two questions were asked using seven-point Likert scales in the manufacturing setting and five-point in services. They were relatively direct and objective assessments consistent with the operationalization grounded in the literature (e.g., Mohr 1971; Glisson 1978; Hrebiniak 1974). These two dimensions of technology were considered conceptually independent and consequently were included separately in the analysis. Table 5A-1 presents the standard score means and standard deviations for the variables in this study.

Analysis of the Data

For the purposes of this investigation the unit of analysis was the individual employee. The individual unit of analysis was decided upon primarily because of Simon's (1957) observation that decisions that are made by individuals must begin with some value premise that is taken as a given. Correlation analysis was undertaken to determine the relationship between individual work values, technology, and structure.

In order to determine whether the dimensions of work values mediated the relationship between structure and technology, hierarchical regression analysis was performed. The latter analysis was also done to assess whether the dimensions of values were related to structure independent of an association they might have with the technological measures (Kerlinger and Pedhazur 1973).

Results

The correlations between each dimension of work values, technology, and structure for both service and manufacturing organizations are presented in Table 5A-2. The results indicate strong correlations between both intrinsic and convenience work values and structure, which were significant beyond the 0.001 level of significance. Generally, when perceived involvement in the decisionmaking process was high, participants reported stronger attachment to their work values. This is consistent with the hypothesis that the value structure of the service provider is positively related to the objective structure of the service firm.

The results in Table 5A-2 provide modest support for an association between values and technology. Both dimensions of work values were significantly ($p < .01$) correlated with task complexity within the services and manufacturing setting. Task integration was not significantly correlated with intrinsic or convenience work values in the service organization sample. Task integration was significantly correlated with both work values dimensions within the manufacturing setting, although in an inverse direction.

The task complexity-work values association seems consistent with the job redesign literature (e.g., Hackman et al. 1975). As job complexity (challenging nonroutine tasks, greater autonomy) increases, the work value attachments of individuals are directly affected. The task integration-work values inverse relationship in manufacturing is probably best explained by the nature of the workflow requirements in this sample of organizations. The assembly line operations required sequential interdependency primarily around the machine task and not any interpersonal relationship task. Low

Table 5A–2. Correlations between Objective Structure, Technology, and Work Value or Subjective Structures.

	Services (N = 620)			Manufacturing (N = 109)				
	ST	TC	TI	IWV	ST	TC	TI	CWV
Structure (ST)	—				—			
Task Complexity (TC)	.22^a	—			.25^b	—		
Task Integration (TI)	-.04	.04	—		-.24^c	-.24^b	—	
Intrinsic Work Values (IWV)	.72^a	.26^a	.14	—	.46^a	.29^a	-.24^b	
Convenience Work Values (CWV)	.61^a	.29^a	.02	.55^a	.53^a	.21^b	-.19^c	.46^a

a. $p < .001$.
b. $p < .01$.
c. $p < .05$.

(or negative) work value attachments are not unexpected in this type of environment, especially with relatively high reorganization of task activities. The same logic applies to the positive (although not significant) task integration-work value relationship in the services setting.

It was also hypothesized that a stronger relationship would be found between work value structures and objective structure in service organizations than in manufacturing organizations. This hypothesis was only partially supported. The difference between the objective structure and intrinsic work value correlation in services was significantly greater than that found in the manufacturing organization ($Z = 3.91$, $p < .001$). However, the objective structure and convenience work value correlation was not significantly different between the two settings ($Z = 1.11$, $p =$ N.S.). This suggests that those work factors external to the person (e.g., working conditions, relations with boss and co-workers) are more equivalently provided for in both organizational settings. The real differences are in terms of the amount of intrinsic work values (e.g., challenge, autonomy). Service organizations thrust the employee into a more active role with the customer/client and correspondingly provide the employee with a greater sense of involvement in the decisionmaking structure.

Subjective or Value Structures as Mediators

The general proposition of this study was that work values would mediate the relationship between structure and technology. In order to test this proposition, as earlier noted, a necessary but not sufficient approach is to show that work values are significantly related to objective structure and technology. The data presented in Table 5A-2 offer this support.

However, Blalock and Blalock (1968) point out that a spurious relationship between the predictor and the dependent variables in which a third variable causes both predictor and dependent variables (e.g., $X \leftarrow Z \rightarrow Y$) is often empirically difficult to distinguish from the situation in which the third variable Z acts as a mediating or intervening variable (e.g., $X \rightarrow Z \rightarrow X$). In order to take into account this possibility, further testing of this proposition was necessary—specificically, a hierarchical regression analysis. This analysis is performed because the introduction of a mediating or intervening variable be-

Table 5A-3. Hierarchical Regression Analysis of Technology and Work Value Dimensions on Objective Structure for Samples Combined ($N = 729$).

	R^2	R^2
Technology	.057	.541
Work Values	.546	.546
$\Delta F_{R^2} = 38.88$[a]	$\Delta F_{R^2} = 3.97$	

a. $p < .001$.

tween the prediction and dependent variable will tend to change the regression coefficient toward zero, suggesting that there is no direct link between the predictor and the dependent variable (Blalock and Blalock 1968).

First, with objective structure as the dependent variable, the technology measures were entered into the regression equation followed by the work value dimensions. Next, a separate regression analysis was conducted with the work value dimensions entering first followed by the technology measures. Data from the entire sample ($N = 729$) were used. The resulting two regressions are shown in Table 5A-3. The partial F-ratios (ΔF_{R^2}) in Table 5A-3 indicate the significance of the additional variance explained by each construct (i.e., technology or work values) when the other construct is already included in the model. The results reveal the work value dimensions making a significant contribution ($p < .001$) to explained variance (50%) in objective structure. Technology does not make significant contribution ($p < .01$) to explained variance beyond that accounted for by the work values dimensions. This would suggest that work values mediate the relationship between objective structure and technology.

In further testing this hypothesis, a hierarchical regression analysis was performed for the two settings (service and manufacturing) separately. The results from these analyses are presented in Table 5A-4. In both the service and manufacturing setting when technology was controlled, work values significantly increased the explained variance in objective structure beyond that accounted for by technology. In the service setting technology failed to increase the variance explained in objective structure when work values were controlled. The inclusion of technology into the regression model in

Table 5A-4. Hierarchical Regression Analysis of Technology and Work Value Dimensions on Objective Structure by Organizational Setting.

	Services	Manufacturing
	R^2	R^2
Technology	.053	.064
Work Values	.587	.359
$\Delta F_{R^2} = 399.67$[a]		$\Delta F_{R^2} = 141.83$
Work Values	.582	.343
Technology	.587	.359
$\Delta F_{R^2} = 3.74$		$\Delta F_{R^2} = 7.69$[b]

a. $p < .001$.
b. $p < .01$.

the manufacturing setting was statistically significant ($p < .01$), although the magnitude of the contribution was negligible ($\Delta_{R^2} = .016$). These findings add some support to the hypothesized mediating effects of values on the relationship between technology and objective structure.

Finally, path analysis was applied to clarify the pattern of causal relations among these variables. As a "decomposition of correlation coefficients," path analysis provided a useful summary of the model and data. The causal model tested proposes that work values influence objective structure and technology and that technology, in turn, also influences objective structure. This is shown in Figure 5A-1.

Following Kerlinger and Pedhazur (1973), we expressed the variables in the model in standardized form (Z scores), and the path coefficients turned out to be standardized regression coefficients (β's) obtained in the ordinary regression analysis. As can be seen in Figure 5A-1, the path coefficient between work values and technology is 0.105, between work values and objective structure 0.714, and between technology and structure -0.043. These results suggest that work values have a strong direct effect on objective structure and a minimal effect on technology. Technology has a negligible direct impact on objective structure in this study.

Subsequent analysis revealed that the two technology dimensions were not significantly correlated in the services sample ($r = .04$,

Figure 5A-1. Path Analysis Model and Coefficients.

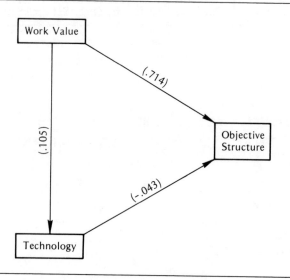

Note: Numbers in parentheses indicate path coefficients.

p = N.S.). They were significantly correlated ($r = -.23, p < .01$) in the manufacturing organization; however, this was not altogether unexpected given the nature of their operations (i.e., assembly line). At the transformation process of such an organization there is low workflow and task uncertainty. In order to optimize the efficiency of the operation, task activities will tend to be sequentially set up. This means there will be a high degree of task interdependence (or integration) required since, for example, activity C cannot be completed before activity B, which in turn is dependent on the completion of activities required. In other words, high task integration and low task complexity should not be unexpected in this type of organization.

6 POWER AND THE ALLOCATION OF RESOURCES WITHIN SERVICES

The production of services is an agency relationship wherein a contract is established under which the client/customer engages the service provider to perform some service on his or her behalf. Thus, contractual relationships are fundamental to the production of services and indeed essential to the very existence of service organizations.

One of the primary functions of service organizations is to satisfy the individualistic and diverse needs of their members. Such membership may consist of suppliers, boards, bankers, stockholders, and so on who may have a vested interest in the firm and who will establish contracts in order to protect that interest. Clearly, the two most important members of service organizations are the employees who contract with the organization to assist in the production of the service and clients/customers who engage the service provider.

Implicit in the contract established between the service organization and its members is a set of mutual expectations involving rights, privileges, and obligations. Such expectations exist not only between the service organization and its employees but also between the organization and clients/customers. The presence of contractual arrangements implies that the parties are exchanging commodities or assets of some value. Thus, service organizations are markets where commodities are exchanged, and contracts serve largely to establish the boundaries around the expectations of those providing the commodities in the exchange (Coase 1952).

Employees and clients/customers of service organizations are in possession of resources or commodities simply because they participate in the production process. The resources may take the form of skills, intelligence, education, effort expended on the job, health, contacts, and so on. In general, these resources are potential "directed effort" around an acceptable skill level and are usually brought to the organization in the form of units of labor time (Leibenstein 1976).

THE NATURE OF THE INTERNAL MARKET

The fact that resources or commodities are exchanged among members within the framework of contracts gives rise to service organizations being "miniature capital markets," as Williamson (1975) has observed. An elementary role of organizations, then, is to facilitate the exchange of scarce resources in the production of the service. The exchange of resources that occurs among the members of service organizations is similar to the exchange that happens in ordinary external marketplaces where consumer-purchased goods and services presumably are governed by the law of supply and demand. What makes the internal markets of service organizations unique is that the exchange is constrained by administrative guidelines and procedures (Doeringer and Piore 1971). The administration of the organization establishes roles for the employees to play. Roles are simply guidelines for expected behavior in accomplishing task activities, for example, how members will interact with others or how much effort one will exert and can expect from others in return. Members (both employees and clients/customers), along with the administrative rules and guidelines, are insulated or protected from external forces. The organization attempts to establish a market system for the relationships among the members based on a relatively independent internal rationality. But such internal rationality is not restricted to governance of relationships. It also affects the pricing of resources and the kinds of mechanisms that will be employed in the allocation of such resources.

In any marketplace there exists the potential for opportunism, that is, self-interest, either by the individual or group, with guile (Williamson 1975). Thus, the rules, regulations, guidelines, and procedures of internal markets also serve to protect the various organization members from each other's predatory tendencies. Such protective mechanisms are not unlike safeguards found in the external marketplace where laws are established to protect the consumer or public from being exploited by unscrupulous sellers of goods and services.

POWER AND ITS ACQUISITION WITHIN INTERNAL MARKETS

We noted in the preceding sections that members of service organizations are in possession of resources simply because they are members. The notion of being a member of an organization implies that one must have a vested interest in the organization and that one has something of value to exchange. The resources that members possess are contained in the individuals' "power bank" (Parsons 1964), or inventory of assets at the disposal of the member for trading with others. Members of service organizations, then, are powerholders because they have valuable commodities that are exchangeable.

The production of services occurs primarily through bilateral exchanges or agency relationships. That is, the internal market relationships or exchanges are creative production processes wherein clients/customers attempt to secure certain resources from the service provider at the cost of giving up others. The service provider may have to give up his or her skill, knowledge, time, or effort in exchange for the client's money, attention, effort in the production process, or satisfaction. In these internal market relationships, resources are being allocated not only between the service employee and clients/customers but also among employees.

Power is an asset utilized by members in their attempt to acquire other assets. We will therefore define power in organizations as the actual or potential ability of members to accumulate valued resources by deliberately affecting the actions of others. This notion of power as an investment phenomenon gives rise to two fundamental aspects of power in organizations. The first aspect is the control over resources. The participant may have education, skills, or contacts that are desired in the exchange. The second aspect of power, which follows from the first, is the control over behavior. This refers to the exchange process in which the powerholder secures resources by having others act in the ways he or she desires.

Clients/customers will give up their money and effort only for the service provider's knowledge, skill, and effort in the production of the service. Further, this exchange of value for value must be undertaken in some fashion such that the eventual outcome leaves the members more satisfied than before the exchange occurred. In other words, resources are important only to the extent that others desire them. Therefore, the general power of members within the internal market of service organizations is dependent on each member's possession of desired resources. This gives rise to an inherent paradox of power in organizations. Control of valued resources gives rise to power in organizations, whereas resources become valued when the interest in them is backed up by power (Hernes 1975).

INTEGRATION OF RESOURCES WITHIN INTERNAL MARKETS

Contracts that are established in the production of services have concomitant costs because parties to the contracts may not always live up to the expectations that generated the contracts. Service providers, for example, may not always act in the clients'/customers' best interest. Thus, clients will be required to expend resources by providing incentives and monitoring activities in order to be assured that agents fulfill their contractual expectations. Jensen and Meckling (1976) refer to these activities as agency costs, or the sum of the client's costs for monitoring the agent's activities, the agent's expenditures for being tied to the clients, and the residual loss in the exchange.

Agency costs will be affected by the mechanisms employed by the organization in integrating or coordinating its resources. Durkheim (1933) conceives of organizations as cooperative systems and suggests a useful taxonomy for the integration of units within organizations. He argues that integration can be accomplished through either "mechanical" or "organic" solidarity. We shall examine these mechanisms as they affect the agency costs of relationships within organizations.

Mechanical Integration

The notion of mechanical solidarity suggests that members within the internal markets of organizations will cooperate only reluctantly due to a perceived disparity in power relationships. Therefore, rules and regulations are set to ensure compliance, and a conflict-oriented state is created. Durkheim notes that mechanical integration is more applicable to situations in which the division of labor is not highly developed or where there is a breakdown in the structure of the organization.

The use of mechanical integration for coordination within internal markets is a temporary state, temporary because it arises from a crisis of conflicts. The presence of conflicts within internal markets implies that the contracts are not being fulfilled. Members have simply refused to accept the guidelines or expectations involved in the exchange.

Perhaps the primary reason that the use of mechanical integration is not in the best interest of the organization, at least over the long run, is that it is inherently conflictual, and its continued use will generate prohibitive costs. Conflicts within internal markets are a gradual escalation to a state of disorder. Consequently, organizations will make an effort to reduce them (Durkheim 1933; Pondy 1967). When conflicts occur between the agents and principals, more resources have to be expended in monitoring activities to enforce the terms of the contract, in renegotiation of contracts, and in setting up incentives in order to ensure compliance. These activities will tend to increase the agency costs, and it is largely for this reason that attempts will be made to reduce conflicts within internal markets.

Organic Integration

When members decide to join an organization, there is an understanding and acceptance of some agreement or contract for cooperation. The idea of becoming a member of an organization is an affirmative activity and an active adjustment to the environment of that organization (Rus 1980). The economic activity within internal markets is mainly due to an inherent recognition of functional interdependence among the members. As a result of this, there is reasonable cooperation among members within the internal markets, and such cooperation will take place in the relative absence of conflicts (Durkheim 1933). In general, as Durkheim notes, cooperative relations do not convey sanctions. Instead they are an accepted form of reciprocity and occur where there is a division of labor. An organic view of solidarity is reflected in a "system of different organs each of which has a special role, and which are themselves formed of differentiated parts" (Durkheim 1933: 181).

In an organization with a high degree of division of labor—for example, organizations engaging in complex activities with much uncertainty surrounding the outcome—participants with activities of dissimilar nature are coordinated and subordinated one to another around some central core. Such a case may be an individual or a department that serves to moderate the activities of the organization. The relationship between the moderating element within the organization and the other participants in the generation of the service is a reciprocal one because there is mutual dependence. Thus power becomes essentially an acceptable exchange of resources.

Since organic solidarity implies some reasonable level of acceptance among members within the internal markets of organizations, it will have a positive effect on the agency costs. The contracts that are established will require fewer resources by principals in monitoring the activities of agents because there will be more cooperation among the participants.

POWER AND EQUITY IN SERVICE TRANSACTIONS

An important element responsible for the efficient operation of the internal market is the law of reciprocity. This is so for the production of services whether the exchange takes place directly between the service employee and client/customer or among employees. The law of reciprocity means that when one party receives something of value from another, the recipient is obliged to return something in kind. Thus, it serves to focus the service performance on the client's/customer's interests.

In the exchanges that occur within service production, reciprocity does not imply equality of the actual resources exchanged. The physical attributes constituting the inputs and outputs to the exchange are different, and the stipulations (implicit or explicit) within the contract may require varying degrees of effort. It is therefore the complementarity of what is exchanged that produces reciprocity, not the equality of the objects exchanged. Thus, a client's/customer's satisfaction with the service provider's effort or know-how in rendering the service is an equitable exchange but not an equal one ("satisfaction" and "contracted service" are clearly not equal in kind). This complementarity is also applicable to relationships among employees involved in the service production. The approval by an authority holder of subordinate compliance is an equitable exchange, but not equal, since "approval" and "ordered work behavior" are not the same in kind. Equitability in these exchanges arises from the mutual agreement that the parties' possessions are of equal value.

What then follows is that differential roles (i.e., special positions in the division of labor) in the production of the service have associated with them differential amounts of power. Given the existence of differential power in a system of functional interdependence, Durkheim's "organic solidarity" becomes the consensus among the members regarding the equity of the normal exchanges that take place within such a system.

THE PRICING OF RESOURCES WITHIN
INTERNAL MARKETS OF SERVICES

When exchanges occur in the production of services, a fundamental assumption is that the sum of values is greater after the transaction than before. By this we mean that each participant in the transaction essentially renders to the other more than he or she previously possessed. A further implication is that before the contracts are agreed upon, values are established for the resources that are inherent in these exchanges. Contracts would not be possible without some predetermined understanding about the value of the resources being exchanged.

In order for an understanding to occur, a pricing mechanism has to exist. The aim of a pricing system within internal markets is to determine the value of resources. This is accomplished by members signaling to each other the kinds of assets (primarily labor skills) that are needed (Doeringer and Piore 1971).

We perceived that power within organizations emerges from the accumulation of valued resources and that these resources are valuable to the degree that others take interest in them. The pricing system is very important within this context because it attempts to convey information about preferences and the costs that will be incurred in order to attain such preferences. When information about the value of resources is available to the participants, the cost involved in establishing contracts will be reduced. The cost reduction occurs in mutually expected behaviors necessary for the establishment of contracts. Thus, the efficiency with which internal markets operate is directly dependent on the pricing system. Since the pricing system is involved in the determination of the value or importance of members' fraction of valued resources, we will address the value of resources in the following sections.

THE VALUATION OF RESOURCES

The contracts established between members of an organization entail two crucial dimensions that affect the value of resources exchanged. One dimension entails the element of uncertainty. The presence of uncertainty in internal market exchanges implies that the issues being addressed are complex, that the parties in the transaction cannot easily discriminate between intended and unintended effects. So many contingencies are possible that it is difficult and very costly to specify in advance what actions will be necessary (Klein 1983).

The second dimension of internal market contracts is the skills or know-how of the agent. When uncertainty is inherent in contracts, the agent's assets that are capable of reducing uncertainty within complex contracts will become valuable. Uncertainty suggests that there are many possible ways, for example, of dealing with the problems of clients/customers with outcomes that are difficult to predict. The fact that uncertainty exists further points to a scarcity of knowledge and ways of solving problems. Those service providers with pertinent skills, knowledge, and experience will be indispensable. These attributes are important because of their potential for addressing specific problems within the internal market.

The value of resources can now be addressed by examining the relationship between the uncertainty around internal market contracts and the agent's skill specificity required to address uncertainty.

Value of Unspecialized Skills
under High Uncertainty

The presence of high uncertainty in contracts suggests that the client's/customer's problems are complex. Complex problems will require an array of possible solutions and can be addressed by the service provider with information or skills that are unspecialized (cell 2 in Figure 6-1). Such information or skills are of a general nature. By this we mean that the service provider possesses a repertoire of possible ways of performing.

Unspecialized information or skills tend to be difficult to obtain. Much sacrifice will be required of the service provider in order to secure a wide array of information. Since contracts with clients will tend to be different, then the value of skills will be directly affected by the vicissitudes of the internal market. By this we mean that such information or skills can be subjected to price discrimination. The service provider in possession of such skills can realize a greater return on his or her investment by varying prices to contracts or problems. Thus, a nonuniform price structure will be geared to each

Figure 6-1. Skill Specificity.

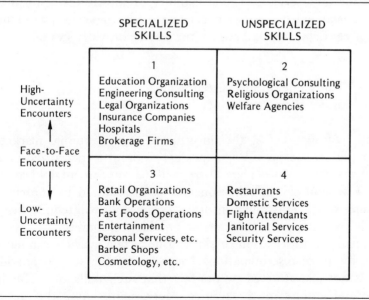

fraction of resources used to provide the service, which increases the incentives for the service provider to secure the client's surplus. When unspecialized skills are required for uncertain contracts, flexible prices generally serve as signals to service providers to continue to invest in developing the skills necessary to keep pace with changing demands.

The Value of Unspecialized Skills under Low Uncertainty

The presence of low uncertainty within service contracts or encounters implies that the client's/customer's problems are not very complex. Few contingencies are needed to address such problems. The service provider can easily specify responses to the client's/customer's problems in advance. Internal service markets that require unspecialized skills to address client's/customer's problems with low uncertainty (cell 4, Figure 6-1) suggest several important things. Although the skill requirement may vary for the service provider, the skills are of a relatively simple nature. They are not difficult to secure, as they do not require much sacrifice by the possessor. The client/customer, in general, can readily find alternative service providers for such services. The availability of substitutes coupled with the relatively small sacrifice needed to secure these skills will tend to keep prices depressed and reduce the service provider's value.

The Value of Specialized Skills under High Uncertainty

In cell 1 of Figure 6-1 the uncertainty of the internal market requires the service provider to possess skills of a specialized nature. For these service providers there will be fundamental exclusivity present around the information and skills required by the client's/customer's problems. Such information or skills will tend to be issue specific and difficult for the service provider to obtain.

Specialized information or skills in uncertain markets can be optimized by price discrimination. The value of the service provider's skills is not just affected by the fact that such skills are difficult to secure and require much sacrifice. More significant is the fact that there is a body of knowledge with relatively good predictability that the service provider can call upon in order to address client/customer problems. The value emerges from the service provider's abilities, skills, and knowledge that enable him or her to reduce the uncertainty surrounding client's/customer's issues.

The Value of Specialized Skills under Low Uncertainty

The internal markets of cell 3 in Figure 6-1 are characterized by little uncertainty and require specialized skills. The problems brought to the organization by clients/customers are simple and specific. It is possible to predict the customer's requests and plan the necessary activities to address such problems. In other words, the operations can be systematized. The service provider must possess skills that are predictable, simple, and narrowly focused on specific issues. This type of situation is quite visible, for example, in the exchanges between cashiers and customers in retail organizations and customers and tellers in banks.

When low-uncertainty internal markets require specific skills to solve problems, there will be interchangeability among service providers. One bank teller can serve a customer as well as another. Generally, any service provider can render the services customers may need. Such interchangeability affects the value of the service provider's skills and information because the availability of substitutes materially reduces the importance of the activities of any particular service provider. Further, such skills will not be readily subjected to internal market price discrimination because they will tend not to differ markedly in nature. It is primarily for this reason that relatively uniform prices will be established for these specific skills and information.

INVESTMENTS WITHIN THE CONSTRAINTS OF CONTRACTS

It was earlier noted that members within the internal markets of services possess power banks or inventories of resources. The assets within the service provider's power bank (bases of power, e.g., authority, expertise, reward, and so on) will have a direct impact on the kinds of contracts the powerholder can negotiate with clients/customers and with other members in the production of the service.

We defined power as the ability to accumulate resources by deliberately affecting the behavior of others. Members within internal markets will engage in the exchange of resources when their assets will increase the overall value of their power banks. Thus, social exchange does not necessarily mean a loss to one of the two parties. From this perspective, the investment potential of the service provider's resources will affect the power bank. Inappropriate application or investment of resources can be very costly to the service provider because resources are assets that can be depleted if they are not invested wisely. For example, a powerholder may use his or her authority as a base of power in order to secure compliance from a subordinate when the use of expertise as a base would have been more appropriate.

The types of investment activity undertaken by the service provider in addressing client's/customer's problems will depend on the nature of the contracts established. When there is uncertainty around the client's/customer's problems, incomplete or relatively vague contracts will have to be established. Since specific information and skills cannot be readily agreed upon, the service provider can undertake relatively more speculative investments in addressing the client's/customer's problems. For example, when a physician advises his or her patient to try a certain drug or new technique, the physician is indeed speculating. The same is true for a lawyer going into litigation for a client or a financial planner mapping out a program for a client.

Although the contracts in these situations may not be specific, they do have zones of acceptance. The zones of acceptance (Simon 1957; Barnard 1938) imply that there are limits to what clients/customers will tolerate, that the investment of the service provider has to fall within certain limits or zones. The more the service provider's investment of information and skills in addressing problems falls outside the client's/customer's zone of acceptance, the greater the risks to the service provider's power bank.

When there is little uncertainty around client's/customer's problems, specific contracts can be established that would entail the skills, information, and energy needed by the service provider. The zones of customer's indifference are relatively narrow, thereby restricting the amount and kind of investments the service provider can engage in and the extent to which the power bank can be enhanced.

THE EXPECTANCY OF OUTCOMES

The service provider's power within internal markets can be viewed as the relationship between what are initially preferred and ultimately realized outcomes in providing the service to clients/customers. Power is a motivational phenomenon and leads inevitably to expectancy theory. This suggests that the tendency to invest and realize a return on that investment is based on the service provider's expectations that the exertion of his or her effort and skills will lead to successful performances, as Figure 6–2 shows. The model further suggests that the service provider has expectations that his or her successful attempts will result in certain outcomes, each with specific gains and costs previously agreed upon with clients/customers.

The service provider will exert some exchange effort in the expectation that such effort will lead to some desired end (for example, that the client/customer will reciprocate by being satisfied, by providing money, or by showing loyalty to the firm) and also based on the perceived valences or attractiveness of the outcome (Vroom 1964; Porter and Lawler 1968).

Service providers will be motivated to exert or invest effort on the client's/customer's behalf if the client's/customer's requests are reasonable and within the service provider's capabilities. The ability to perform the activities necessary to render the service generates a first-level outcome for the service provider. In other words, the service provider's effort was responsible for solving the client's/customer's problems.

Figure 6–2. Power Expectancy Model.

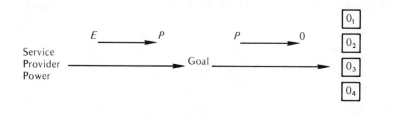

But the service provider's motivation to exert effort for the client/ customer will be enhanced significantly if desirable consequences for the ensuing performance are realized—if the service provider was rewarded with money, client/customer loyalty, client/customer satisfaction, and so on. These are second-level outcomes because they emerge from having rendered a deed for the client/customer. The influence within the exchange is reciprocal. If the client/customer views the expected exchange—that is, the service provider's effort or performance—as inequitable, there will be less compliance with the contract, and then the service provider must bear the loss of compliance.

The expectancy model suggests that the use of the service provider's assets or power is dependent on the reciprocal instrumentality of the client's/customer's compliance in leading to some other outcomes. The perceptions of the service provider's skills, abilities, and information will influence expectancy-performance ($E \to p$) estimates. For example, if the clients/customers expect the service provider to influence their behavior through reasonable exchanges of resources, then the service provider may have a higher perceived probability of cooperation.

SUMMARY

Service organizations are markets set up to facilitate the exchange of resources between the service provider and clients/customers. Within these internal markets members are in possession of assets, which are maintained in power banks. Members within the internal markets are driven by self-interest to optimize their resources through what is perceived to be equitable exchange. The service provider can deplete or enhance his or her power bank based on the appropriateness of the investment. Much of the conflict that emerges between the service provider and client/customer can be explained by the perceived inequity in the contract established between these participants.

7 MANAGERIAL CONTROL OF PERFORMANCE

When people become employees of service organizations, a fundamental agreement is established between the employee and the organization—an agency relationship. By this we mean that the service organization contracts with the employee to perform a service on its behalf. In so doing, there is a transference of property rights in which the employee leases his or her effort, knowledge, skills, information, experience, and so on to the hiring organization.

One realistic and meaningful way to view the contract between the service employee and the service organization is within the context of a franchise relationship wherein the organization is the franchiser and the employee becomes the franchisee. From this perspective, the service organization has some service output that is for sale and contracts with the employee franchisee to dispense or market this service to clients/customers. Thus, the fact that contracts exist means that the organization requires a certain amount of conformity or control as a means for the integration of activities.

As franchisees, service employees often undertake activities that are in situations where it is difficult to monitor performance and behavior. This is especially so in situations involving direct interaction with clients/customers. For example, loan officers operate alone with clients, tellers see customers alone, teachers interact with students alone, and social case workers see clients alone. Further, employees may simply not always act in the best interest of the organization to which their services are leased. Consequently, it benefits the organization to develop control mechanisms that provide the employee with incentives to perform efficiently.

CONTROL AT THE PRIMARY OPERATING CORE

Control is a fundamental managerial process. Within organizations activities are broken down by the division of labor into varied roles to be performed by people. The control process assists in the necessary integration of the diverse behaviors emerging from these varied roles, occupational groups, and functional specialists that result from the division of labor (McMahon and Ivancevich 1971). Control in service organizations is basically achieved through guidelines, which may or may not be formally established by members of the organization (Clegg 1981).

We will define managerial control as a process by which those in authority positions determine what others will do. The process entails a set of activities necessary to ensure that the sought after performance achieves intended and desired organization goals and outcomes. The control activities may include planning, setting up incentive systems to prevent shirking and to motivate employees to perform, coordinating activities both within and across departments, and monitoring and taking corrective action when necessary.

Although these control activities may be pervasive at all levels of the service organization—that is, at the strategic apex, the middle management, and the operating core—each level will tend to emphasize different activities within the set. Our discussion of managerial control will be limited to the primary operating core, based on the notion that service organizations exist to produce a service, and the primary operating core is where this is actually done.

CONTROLLING PRODUCTIVE BEHAVIOR

An important element in employee productivity is the cost incurred. Employee productivity is a function of costs relative to prices. Productivity gains can be realized through cost controls. Such controls are especially important for services because these organizations are generally labor intensive and their operations do not readily lend themselves to economies of scale.

Within services, production is a function of the fit between employees and the tasks they have to perform. The greater the match between what the worker has to do and his or her capabilities, the greater the performance. At the operating core of these organizations, much of the required task activities centers around the demands of clients/customers.

The production of the service output involves uncertainty. Thus, the resources of the workforce within the primary operating core will tend to be heterogenous. These employees will possess varied sets of skills, abilities, and talents. Performance can only be ensured when the service employee has the requisite abilities, skills, and training as well as a thorough understanding of what the job entails and what is expected.

In order to match the service employee to task activities, especially the critical matching up of employee to clients/customers, much information about the employee will have to be secured. The more information managers can obtain about an employee's capabilities the better equipped the manager will be to assign tasks. The most crucial source of an employee's abilities is his or her work history or performance on previously assigned task activities. Such task activities essentially serve as "screening tasks" (Prescott and Visscher 1980), and they provide vital information about the employee's potential.

The set of activities in an employee's screening tasks will tend to be complex largely because of its variety, and the information regarding the employee's performance will be equivocal. The extent to which the information generated by the screening tasks is meaningfully received is a function of the manager's perception of the employee. Managers apply interpretation schemes to such information. If their interpretation schemes are awkward or faulty, there is a possibility for misinterpretation, which could have adverse cost effects.

Three types of information regarding employee performance in screening tasks can be of assistance to the manager: consistency, consensus, and distinctiveness (Kelley 1967). Consistency information provides the relative stability of the employee's performance over time on previously assigned tasks. Consensus information affords the manager an opportunity to compare the performance of one employee with that of others. Distinctiveness information provides a basis for comparing the employee's performance on one set of task activities with his or her performance on a different set of task activities.

The richness of the information on employee performance that is generated by the screening task will be heavily dependent on the length of tenure employees have in these activities. The longer the time an employee spends in screening tasks the better it is for the manager to evaluate performance. A critical factor that influences the amount of time an employee will remain in screening tasks is the rate of growth of the firm. When the organization is growing rapidly there is a greater need for labor. Consequently, employees must be promoted more rapidly from screening tasks to other productive activities. This means that the manager will be forced to make task assignments based on relatively less information about employees, thus increasing the likelihood of making a poor match between the service employee and the task assigned, which will further increase costs through poor performance.

When the service organization is growing slowly, a better quality of information can be obtained by observing employees for longer periods of time in screening tasks. Thus, the organization saves on adjustment costs, as better measures of the employee's abilities, skills, and capabilities can be more readily ascertained (Prescott and Visscher 1980).

MONITORING MECHANISMS

Managerial control implies not only the assignment of the right employee to the right task but also methods of monitoring such activities. Cost reduction can be realized when there is a fit between the monitoring techniques and the nature of the task activities.

There are two basic monitoring mechanisms available to managers in the operations of service organizations: output and behavior or process control (Ouchi and Maguire 1975). The degree of uncertainty inherent in the employee's task activities will determine the monitoring mechanism used. When there is high uncertainty, the relationship between cause and effect is reduced, as there are many possibilities in arriving at the desired outcome. It is therefore difficult for the manager to determine beforehand just how the task activities should be performed. The manager will have to look at the output or results in order to determine the employee's performance.

When there is little uncertainty around the task activities, it is possible to preplan and determine how the activities should be performed. Systems can be developed and the manager can monitor the process and the specific behaviors of the employee in order to determine performance. In process control written records are established for evaluating and detecting deviations for corrective action.

As one moves away from the operating core, especially at the middle management and the strategic apex, other monitoring mechanisms will be used, primarily the budget and statistical reports. The budget serves as a means to control the way that resources, both human capital and physical capital, are allocated according to priorities. Statistical reports provide information on output or how well performance is adhering to established standards (Daft and Macintosh 1984).

EMPLOYEE SELF-CONTROL

In order for managerial control to be cost effective there must be a congruence among the amount of managerial monitoring, the nature of the task environment, and the employees' ability to control themselves. When there is high uncertainty present in the workflow and task activities there will be less need to monitor the employees' activities, as it is difficult to determine what actions should be taken beforehand. The specific situations will generally determine the appropriate actions, meaning that the employee will have to be allowed much discretion. In other words, the manager will have to give up control to employees so that the latter become responsible for managing themselves.

Employee self-supervision reduces costs as activities traditionally reserved for managers are taken over by subordinate employees. The conventional notion of managers instructing subordinates in task-related activities and requiring adherence to prescribed rules and procedures are not generally present in the self-managed state. There is managerial cost savings in this control measure because employees are allowed to perform many of the activities traditionally reserved for managers such as the selection of work techniques, interactions with clients/customers, and work standard variance (Slocum and Simms 1980; Mills and Posner (1982).

Although in the self-controlled state control is actually being delegated to subordinates, managers still have important activities to execute. The role of the manager will focus on two sets of activities concerning the organization's performance. One role is to provide support to employees. There is usually high workflow and high task uncertainty in situations calling for employee self-control, and the information being processed by employees will tend to be equivocal, ambiguous, or uncertain. Employees attempt to employ bounded rationality with such information—that is, transform equivocal information into degrees of equivocality with which the individual can work. This attempt to render the equivocal information unequivocal entails the use of equivocal task procedures (Weick 1969). In addition, the employee will be very uncertain about his or her performance because there is no guarantee that the procedures used will remove equivocality from the information and be of benefit to the client/customer. Further, in situations calling for self-control there is usually a lapse between the time the employee takes action and the time the effects of that action are realized. These factors—uncertainty about outcomes and the length of time for feedback—will tend to create anxiety for the employee. Managers can reduce such anxiety by providing the employee assurance, support, concern, and consideration. In these situations the manager has a delicate role. As a conduit to upper management policy, the manager must provide the necessary autonomy, must be available, but must never be perceived as an overbearing presence. The manager is more of a resource than a watchman.

The other role for the manager in self-controlled situations is to redefine the subordinate's zones or boundaries of authority, which are constantly shifting. The delegation of control to subordinates is a negotiated process. This is because the amount of control delegated to employees has to match the situation and the employees' abilities to handle such control. When there is incongruence between the employees' ability to use the control and the amount of control rendered to the situation, costs can be expected to increase. There are two possibilities here: one is the underdelegation of control and the other is the overdelegation of control to employees (Bazerman 1982).

In the underdelegation of control there is incongruence because the employee is allowed less control over the task activity than his or her ability to use such control. The employee has a sufficient set of methods and alternatives from which to draw in addressing issues but is severely restricted in doing so. This increases costs because employees are restricted in how their tasks will be completed. Further, it results in duplication of effort because managers tend to become too closely involved in subordinates' activities.

In the overdelegation of control there is incongruence because the employee is given more control over the task activity than he or she has the ability to make use of. In this situation the employee has a sufficient number of alternatives and methods from which to choose but is limited by his or her abilities in evaluating such alternatives. This type of incongruence has an adverse effect on performance.

CONTROL LOSS

Employee compliance in the pursuit of goals and outcomes cannot always be ensured. In fact, very often employees will not comply with the requests or desires of managers in service operations. In this event there is a loss of control. The notion of control loss in the service operations, then, is the extent to which the subordinate fails to carry out the intentions of the manager. Control loss implies managerial inefficiency because there is a failure to obtain subordinates' compliance that adversely affects the operations (Evans 1975).

Managers are less likely to experience control loss where there is little task and workflow uncertainty. In these situations it is possible to predict and preplan the activities necessary to secure the desired outcome. Managers can employ behavior control or process control over the activities performed by subordinates and minimize control loss through systems with built-in mechanisms to detect deviations and take corrective actions. The more the employee's behavior is determined by others the less leeway that employee will have in determining his or her course of action.

Control loss is more likely to occur where high uncertainty surrounds task and workflow activities. Within this context it is difficult to determine beforehand what actions will be necessary to address issues and outcomes that are contingent on the employee's performance. Since there may be many methods an employee can use to solve problems, there is a need for discretion and the delegation of control. Such autonomy can stimulate independent thinking among subordinates that may deviate from the manager's intentions.

Managerial inefficiency that emerges from control loss can be reduced if three fundamental elements are present. First, if employees understand what they are supposed to be doing and possess the abilities and resources to do it, they will be more willing to carry out the manager's requests. Second, employees must perceive an association between the effort they exert and performance. That is, they have to feel that their efforts will produce some desired results. Finally, employees must perceive an association between performance and valued outcomes, for example, pecuniary reward, promotion, or recognition.

Further reduction in control loss can be realized based on the employee's perception of the manager. A manager has to be perceived as influential with his or her own superior to be influential with his or her own subordinates. When employees detect that their immediate superiors have little influence with higher level managers, they are less likely to comply.

CONTROLLING CLIENT/CUSTOMER PERFORMANCE IN THE DIRECT ENCOUNTER WITH THE FIRM

When clients/customers contract with service organizations to render a service on their behalf, the contract involves delegating some decisionmaking authority to the service provider. Patients hire doctors and give them certain rights to tell the patients what to do. This is simply the nature of how services are rendered. It is inherent in service contracts that clients/customers have important task activities to perform in service operations (Rosengren and Lefton 1975). Patients keep records of symptoms to be relayed to their physicians; clients keep records of expenditures to be given to their tax accountants; students do homework and prepare for classes and exams. We have earlier argued that because of the clients'/customers' direct face-to-face encounter with service employees, the clients/customers are more accurately viewed as "partial" employees. Operating costs can be saved when clients'/customers' activities are controlled, as fewer disruptions in the operations will occur.

It is important to realize that by delegating some decisionmaking right to the service provider the client/customer has given authority to the service provider. This is a basic characteristic of service contracts. As partial employees, clients/customers enter the encounter as subordinates to the full-time service employees. Thus, there is a disparity in status based on the legitimate rights bestowed on the service employee as a franchisee of the organization in the production and as the dispenser of the service to the client/customer. Disparity in power may also emerge from the monopolization of knowledge, expertise, or information possessed by service employees (Friedson 1970).

When clients/customers enter into the service operations as temporary members they become the responsibility of the service employee. The service employees at the encounter then can be viewed as first line managers for the organization, responsible for the coordination and control of the activities of clients/customers in the exchange. The managerial control approach employed by the service employee in these face-to-face interactions with clients/customers is a function of the type of encounter. Two possible managerial approaches that an employee can undertake are "supervision" and "leadership." Supervision occurs when the individual secures compliance from the subordinate through the possession of authority, that is, legitimate or positional power. Leadership occurs, on the other hand, when the individual secures compliance from the subordinate by means other than resorting to one's authority or position.

In encounters with low-uncertainty service operations (bank tellers, barbers, domestics, flight attendants, etc.) where contracts between the service provider and clients/customers are specific and in which the task activities required of these participants are relatively routine, a supervision control will be most efficient. In these interactions what clients/customers are required to do in the service operations is relatively predictable. This makes it possible to preplan for these activities; consequently, rules and regulations can be established to govern client/customer behavior. The service employees have the authority to enforce such rules and regulations. For example, queuing arrangement is often employed by service organizations in order to deal with more than one customer at a time. This "first come first serve" rule produces an ordering procedure for the operation. If a consumer breaks this rule and causes disruption in the queue, the service employee has the authority to restore order by enforcing the rule. Thus, in low-uncertainty encounters the influence of customers involves the service employee's resorting to authority derived from the specificity of the service contract.

Conversely, in high-uncertainty service operations, the encounters with clients/customers will be relatively complex and the contracts established between the service providers and their clients/customers will not be very specific. The task activities required of these clients/customers are of a relatively complex nature, prohibiting preplanning. There is a need for novel solutions since new situations invariably emerge with each contact episode. Consequently, the service contract will have to be of a general nature with much discretion at the disposal of the members. Consumers' compliance will be accomplished through employee leadership. Service employees will attempt to influence their clients/customers to perform efficiently by employing resources that are not only outside the legitimate position of the service contract but also primarily anchored in the interpersonal exchanges.

CONTROL OF CLIENT PERFORMANCE THROUGH PROFESSIONAL DISTANCE

The notion of controlling client/customer performance through leadership mechanisms has important cost implications for the service operation. The operation must determine the form such a control mechanism must take in order to be cost effective. In other words, the issue centers around the most effective leadership mode employees should adopt in rendering the service directly to clients/customers.

It has long been recognized that the performance and behavior of clients/customers can be influenced when the service provider displays "social distance," which is a barrier between the service provider and clients/customers, based on status. Service employees in direct encounters with clients can make more reasonable, objective decisions and produce more effective service when they maintain social distance with customers. However, social distance also carries a potential loss of understanding that could result in inefficient exchanges between the service provider and the clientele. For example, physicians who use medical jargon to distance themselves from their patients have been found to be less successful in producing health in their patients than communicative physicians (Korsch and Negreta 1972).

The exchanges in service encounters can be optimized when "professional distance" is practiced in the relationship between service employees and their clients/customers. Professional distance is an impersonal interest is the affairs of clients/customers. Renee Fox's (1959) notion of "detached concern" captures the essence of professional distance. Here the service employee shows some subjective interest in the client, which fosters understanding of the underlying issues and simultaneously displays an objective detachment for making reasonable decisions in efficiently rendering the service.

Professional distance is quite different from social distance. Social distance is largely a state of aloofness toward the client/customer. Professional distance is a more complex mechanism that entails, on the one hand, concern or empathy for the flow of crucial information and better understanding and, on the other hand, some detachment for objective decisionmaking.

It is possible that service providers in direct encounters with clients/customers may indeed experience some affective reality. But such emotion should be controlled in an attempt to enhance the employee's equanimity and maintain a balance between an empathetic and a relatively objective understanding.

Although professional distance may be useful in all service operations where clients/customers are directly involved, it is especially pertinent to those operations where there is high uncertainty, where the activities necessary to render the service are complex, and where cause-effect relations are difficult to determine. Much trial and error is required of the service employees in these situations, as there can be little reliance on past procedures. Since the process of trial and error is inherent in these service operations, clients will not readily comply with the service employee's requests. Client compliance will be more forthcoming where there is trust and respect for the service provider. The intention of professional distance is to foster such client respect for the service provider and in so doing secure the former's compliance.

One way that professional distance can be established is for the service employee to be task oriented, that is, to concentrate primarily on the task activities at hand and to maintain impartiality. It is also important for the service provider to maintain the status distinction through the legitimate position bestowed upon him or her by the client in establishing the contract. One benefit of professional distance in the performance of service operations is that clients find it easier to criticize the service provider when the latter is not living up to contract expectations. The process of criticism serves as an invaluable mechanism for completing contract negotiations. When clients have difficulty criticizing service providers, the exchange is not only perceived as inequitable but accepted as such and thus, over time, adversely affects client compliance. Further, by being close to the client, the service provider has not only reduced his or her legitimate status but has also depreciated his or her expertise as an exchange commodity. It will therefore be difficult for the service provider to exert the legitimate power or authority should such a necessity arise.

There may be temporary gain in a situation in which a close association is allowed to develop between the service provider and clients/customers. Closeness in encounters can indeed reduce transaction costs. When the client finds an atmosphere that is supportive and a service provider that is approachable, he or she can behave in a relatively nonthreatening environment. Further, close interaction increases the status of the client by creating an egalitarian relationship.

However, there are potential long-term adverse cost effects to the service operation from such short-term gains. In return for emotional support, a client is likely to be loyal to the service provider. There would then be a reluctance to blame the service employee when poor service is being administered because the client's act of criticizing reduces the legitimate or authority position of the service provider. Such an act would be unnecessary since the service provider, by being close to the client, has already not only reduced his or her legitimate status but also depreciated his or her expertise as an exchange commodity.

Professional distance may be crucial to the effective performance of the service operation in another respect. In many service operations where there is high uncertainty—for example, psychiatry, jury trials, religious organizations, and brokerage firms—the techniques for solving clients' problems generally have very limited cause-effect predictability. Moreover, since the service is of a psychological nature, there are limited ways of determining its effectiveness. Consequently, the client must have a certain amount of "faith" in the information and abilities of the service provider. This faith, which is often an irrational belief in the improbable, is crucial to secure the desired results. Professional distance is partially capable of enhancing trust by creating an aura of mystery around the service provider, thus elevating his or her status position and thereby increasing the likelihood of client compliance.

SUMMARY

It seems clear that control in service organizations is complicated by the inclusion of clients/customers in the operations. The notion of performance in the primary operating core of service organizations is not restricted to the service employee but also includes the activities performed by clients/customers.

Performance of service providers at the primary core can usually be optimized when there is a fit between the kinds of services required of the employee and his/her capabilities. For managers to make such a fit, much information must be obtained about the employee. Crucial information about an employee's potential can be secured through screening tasks.

Although output and process control may be implemented to control performance in service operations, self-control will also be pervasive. Self-control mechanisms will be employed more extensively as the client's/customer's involvement increases. In such situations, managers will still have a vital role to play in providing the authority for discretion and the support to the service employee that will enhance his or her effectiveness.

The control of client/customer performance in service operations is more problematic. One way that managers can assure client/customer performance is by encouraging service providers to practice professional distance, especially in high-encounter situations. One important benefit of professional distance is that it can also be aligned with the quality of service delivered as clients/customers may actually come to expect such behavior from service providers.

8 THE QUALITY OF SERVICES DELIVERED

When clients/customers contract with service organizations for the service output, they are actually bargaining for direct performance or effort with the organizations' employees. Since the output of services is so entwined with the service provider's efforts, an important issue for service organizations is the quality level at which employees perform. The quality issue directly affects the productivity of these organizations (Klaus, 1985). The productivity of the service provider can be viewed as the volume of services per capita that is generated by each member within the organization. It is the value of output produced by the service provider relative to the value of what it costs the service provider to produce the output.

Productivity of the service provider consists of two fundamental aspects: efficiency and effectiveness. Efficiency is concerned with the operational-type activities—those activities involved in the conversion of input into output or the resources involved in the generation of finished services. Effectiveness, on the other hand, is concerned with the impact of the finished services on the intended client/customer—with the consequences or the results of the operational activities (Mark 1981). Organization effectiveness examines whether the optimum use of resources was employed in the achievement of the service output. Effectiveness is determined by the quality of service that is produced when quality or effectiveness of the service output is taken within the context of the effort being exerted by service employees. This becomes quite problematic for the service organization and its clients or customers.

CAVEAT EMPTOR — LET THE CUSTOMER BEWARE

The quality or effectiveness of a service that is rendered to clients/customers is difficult to determine. Service output is essentially intangible, which renders the effectiveness of such output an abstraction that cannot be observed directly. Further, the effectiveness of the service is inherently subjective because it is so difficult to measure (Cameron 1981). This is particularly so for services where much uncertainty surrounds the production of the output.

Since the service organization sells an effort or performance under conditions of varying degrees of uncertainty, the quality and quantity of output cannot be objectively determined. The client/customer is vulnerable to the service provider, who is in a position to bargain opportunistically, that is, display self-interest with guile. As a result, clients and customers have to be aware of two opportunistic procedures that the service provider might undertake: "adverse selection" and "moral hazard."

Adverse selection emerges when the client/customer is unable to observe and monitor the activities being performed by the service provider. The client can observe neither the service provider's characteristics nor the contingencies under which the provider operates. It is very difficult, for example, for patients to determine whether the tests and treatments administered by the physician are appropriate. Consequently, there is adverse selection or the temptation of the service provider to oversupply the service. Clients of legal firms can be billed for an inordinate amount of hours whether or not the billable time was actually expended productively in the client's best interest.

Moral hazard is fostered when the quality and quantity of the service being rendered to clients/customers are difficult to verify. In such situations, standards become meaningless. For example, although an attorney may devote an enormous amount of effort in litigation on a client's behalf, there is no guarantee that the case will be successful. The client will be uncertain whether an unfavorable outcome was due to insufficient effort by the attorney or just happenstance. Since effort is difficult to measure, there is a temptation for the service provider to undersupply it unless incentives are provided to encourage proper service or effort (Holstrom 1982).

Moral hazard and adverse selection reduce the value or quality of the service consumed by clients/customers. This is so even when attempts are made to place a ceiling on the services being rendered. For example, instituting fixed prices for some Medicaid services is an attempt to deal with the adverse selection problem by restricting the services available to these patients. This means that highly desired resources are not made available to clients/customers. Unfortunately, even in such restricted situations moral hazard and adverse selection can still occur. Since the patient cannot observe or determine what activities are appropriate, the fixing of prices or setting of a price ceiling on health care will be an incentive to restrict the services being rendered. By reducing the amount of services under such conditions, the service provider is in fact inflating the price of those resources that are actually exchanged. Thus, the quality of the service rendered to clients is adversely affected.

There are two fundamental mechanisms for reducing the loss in the value or quality of the service provided to clients and customers due to adverse selection and moral hazard: monitoring and bonding activities.

MONITORING ACTIVITIES

Monitoring activities are those activities undertaken by clients/customers to reduce the loss of quality in services caused by the moral hazard and adverse selection problems associated with the service provider. Monitoring activities include the time and effort required of clients/customers to assure that the service provider adheres to contractual stipulations.

Due Diligence

Due diligence entails the time spent learning about the skills required to perform the task and interviewing potential service providers in order to obtain second opinions. This process is quite common, for example, with medical and financial services.

Due diligence is intended to protect clients and customers from poorly trained, poorly supervised, and unscrupulous service providers. It does not guarantee that the services being rendered by, for example, the physician or the investment adviser, will be successful. Rather, it increases the confidence of the client/customer that there is a good probability that the services being rendered will have their intended effects.

Effort Substitutions

In general, monitoring activities increase as the uncertainty around the production of the service increases. Assessing the quality of the performance of the service provider becomes problematic for the consumer as the difficulty of determining specific performance outcomes increases. The consumer's inability to attribute inputs readily to specific outputs reduces the effectiveness of monitoring inputs as a means of controlling performance. Thus, the consumer may substitute the provider's degree of effort as a measure for assessing performance. But this approach has limited effectiveness for situations in which the correlation between input and output is low (e.g., legal and medical services, consulting services) because the client's ability to understand the activities involved in the production of such complex services is reduced and the cost of acquiring the skills needed to monitor performance is high. In other words, the more complex the service encounter, the more costly will be the monitoring methods required.

BONDING ACTIVITIES

Bonding activities are incurred by the service firm in order to ensure some minimum level of performance. Whereas monitoring activities reduce the resources acquired by the firm through reduced selling prices for services, bonding activities reduce the firm's resources through increased operating costs. However bonding activities undertaken by the firm supplant the need for the client/customer to incur monitoring activities or costs.

Typical bonding activities include those activities associated with obtaining and displaying credentials (e.g., CPA, MD, MBA). This acquisition of degrees, certificates, and professional associations is an important process of licensing, and it indicates that the service provider has external sources that are engaged in scrutinizing his or her activities. Other bonding activities may be incurred by developing goodwill (institutional advertising, community involvement) and offering guarantees.

The Importance of Reputation

The primary intention of the bonding mechanisms is to enhance the service provider's reputation. For the service provider, reputation credibility is a valuable asset. Because the buyer cannot confidently determine the service that is rendered even after it is purchased, the client/customer must rely on the reputation of the service provider for a repeat purchase. For example, a patient cannot usually evaluate the competence of the physician after one visit for the treatment of one complaint, but must secure the perception of such competence from other sources. In essence, the reputation of the firm signals to the client that there is reliable and valuable information about expected performance.

Service organizations can facilitate the bonding process by disclosing information about their performance to potential customers. For example, health care organizations can disclose information about fees, death rates for patients in that hospital, and the percentage of successful operations relative to mean rates; education institutions can disclose information about student placements after matriculation; and legal firms can provide information about settlements in disputes, litigation won and lost, and so on.

The disclosure of this kind of information will increase colleague or peer monitoring within the organization. One incompetent employee can adversely affect the reputation of others within the workflow. In order to protect their reputations, members within the organization will be apprehensive to report incompetent colleagues. When companies fail to disclose information about their performance to potential customers, they risk reducing the quality of their service output because they reduce the incentive for members within the organization to monitor the activities of their colleagues. Since the reputation of the firm is perceived as not being an issue, there will be very little motivation for members to expose incompetent colleagues. Indeed, there may even be an incentive to protect the incompetent in such situations. For example, physicians may be reluctant to reveal an incompetent colleague for fear of potential law suits.

Ideological Similarity

To a significant degree, bonding activities and their accompanying costs are a function of trust. The less the client/customer trusts the service provider the more the latter must rely on his or her own expenditures to reduce expected loss in quality of service. One important way trust in the encounter may be affected is by ideological similarity (Bachrach and Lawler 1980). Ideological similarity suggests that the parties to the exchange are less likely to adhere to the stipulations of the contract when they are ideologically opposed. This can occur when providers are not fastidious about attracting and selecting clients/customers with attitudes, values, and expectations that are consistent with their own attitudes, values, and abilities.

The type of bonding activities employed will be dependent on what most effectively encourages adherence to the stipulations of the contract, which in turn is a function of the uncertainty of the production of the service output. When the services being rendered can be stipulated and are relatively measurable—for example, being served in a fast food restaurant or passing a real estate exam—a money-back guarantee may drastically reduce deviations from expected behaviors. Conversely, when there is high uncertainty around the output of the service (e.g., in brokerage firms and penal institutions) assessing successful performance is more difficult and guarantees are inappropriate.

THE FUNDAMENTALS OF QUALITY SERVICE PROVIDER BEHAVIOR

Clearly, it is easier to measure the quality of goods produced by a manufacturing organization than it is to measure the quality of output produced by service organizations. Since the production of most services entails some interaction between the service provider and clients/customers, there is increased difficulty in measuring the quality of the outcome. The interaction in the production process subjects the service output to errors because people engaged in such interactions work in environments where many factors contribute to the potential for making errors. Since there are many ways to generate the service output, and there is a propensity for people to make mistakes, it is not unreasonable to expect a large number of errors in the production of services (Adam et al. 1981).

The transmissions from the service provider to the client/customer are of two types: technical skills and social or interpersonal skills. Technical skills are peculiar to a specific profession or kind of service, and the possession of such skills gives the service provider his or her expertise in that area. The service provider has a body of laws and paradigms capable of addressing issues peculiar to his or her field (e.g., knowledge in medicine, law, or real estate).

The social or interpersonal side of the service is the nontechnical dimension. This is the service orientation, and it entails a set of attitudes and behaviors by the service provider that affect the quality of the interaction with clients/customers. The importance of service orientation skills is well recognized. In the health care profession, for example, the bedside manner of the health care provider is generally acknowledged to be an important element in the quality of care of patients (Hogan, Hogan, and Busch 1984).

We have noted in Chapter 2 that in the social interaction between the service provider and clients there are some basic mutual understandings. Clients/customers usually expect that the same or equal service will be dispensed with little or no favoritism. There is also the expectation that clients/customers will be treated with courtesy (Goffman 1983). In other words, gestures and manners indicate approval of the client's presence in the interaction and that the service provider finds such interaction pleasurable. Further, the service provider's actions indicate tact and perception about the client's needs.

Although we have drawn a distinction between the technical skills and service-orientation skills, this distinction is largely for analytical purposes. Both skills are interdependent and necessary contributors to the quality of service rendered.

THE EFFECTS OF SERVICE ORIENTATION
ON QUALITY

The personal interaction in the production of services is basically a function of the amount of information passed from the service provider to the client/customer. Of course, in order for transmission to occur effectively information must be secured from the client/customer. But the ultimate goal of the interaction is to provide information in order to solve problems. Salient in interaction is the set of technical skills possessed by the service provider.

The "relational" nature of the interaction between the service provider and the client/customer brings into sharp focus the inevitable and vital service-orientation dimension, the crucial role played by the attitudes of the service provider in the transmission of his or her technical skills to the client/customer. The service provider cannot communicate technical skills to clients/customers independent of his or her service orientation or set of attitudes toward the client/customer. This is because attitude is an integral aspect of any interpersonal communication process.

The service orientation or attitude toward the client/customer can be viewed as the inner state of the provider and entails the things subjectively perceived (Homans 1950). Attitudes are the overt manifestation of things intrinsically valuable or desirable to the service provider and may further reflect the value structure within the service organization.

Since values serve as a rationale for people's behavior, any flow of information between the service provider and clients/customers is invariably accompanied by much more than what is deliberately intended. The attitudes of the parties involved in the interaction are also conveyed either by the service provider's manner or the context of the situation.

Thus, the quality of the service output cannot be realized without regard to the service provider's attitudes or service orientation. The receptivity of the client/customer to the technical skills of the service provider is dependent on the latter's service orientation or interpersonal skills. The service provider's technical skills and attitude toward the client/customer evolve together on the basis of the interaction. A service provider with an arrogant, hostile, or negative attitude toward the client/customer will certainly be more likely to distort or hinder the transmission of technical information than will a provider with a positive, friendly attitude. It is primarily within this context that Simon (1957) long ago recognized that congenial attitudes should be maintained in order to foster interaction and efficient operations. Increased positive attitudes and the flow of information are highly correlated (Gellerman 1968) and easily permeate the boundaries separating the service provider and the client/customer. The extent to which a customer will remain with a service organization is very dependent on the attitude of the service provider with whom they directly interact.

TOWARD THE DEVELOPMENT OF QUALITY SERVICE

Quality service has been equated with the notion of effectiveness, that is, the consequences of the service being rendered to clients/customers. Because the consequences of service output may generate many versions of reality in service markets, service organizations cannot be the sole judge of their own effectiveness (Jobson and Schneck 1982). Service organization effectiveness is a multidimensional if not subjective concept. Shostack's (1977) notion of "consensus realities," where behavior or task performance is compared not only with internal criteria but also with external criteria as perceived by clients and customers, is meaningful in this context.

Consensus reality is crucial for service organization effectiveness in another way as well. Organizations are in a constant tradeoff between externally defined criteria of effectiveness and internally defined criteria. Generally, these perspectives of effectiveness are incompatible, partially because of the differences in the kinds of indicators used to reflect the two criteria. Service organizations tend to use subjective indicators usually constructed from surveys of clients and customers about their experiences and perceptions of the services received. These are then contrasted with objective internal indicators. It is little wonder that the two are incongruent. Parks (1984) has noted that the internal indicators of effectiveness are essentially measures of input, and the external input of clients/customers is largely subjective measures of outcomes. It is for this reason that studies have found the satisfaction level of clients/customers with the services to be totally independent of the actual level of service provided (Stipak 1979).

VICARIOUS CONSUMPTION BY CLIENTS

Often clients/customers may not be totally aware of the actual level and kinds of services they have received. What is therefore expressed by these consumers may not accurately reflect the service being rendered. Further, clients/customers may actually have "vicarious" experience about a service. That is, they may not have actually consumed or experienced the service but learned about it from peers, media, and observations and then developed subjective perceptions (Skogan and Maxfield 1981). It would seem prudent for the service organization to bring its objective internal criteria in line with the tendency of clients and customers to employ subjective evaluations. However, the service organization should be aware that clients and customers evaluate the effectiveness of services rendered on the basis of what they consider to be desirable (values) and not necessarily what is desired (goals). Since desired factors are subject to change in response to changing situations, a more stable and consistent basis for evaluating the organization's effectiveness should be determined (Cameron 1981).

In order to examine the effectiveness or quality issue, the service organization must be concerned with three basic aspects of the service being provided: the structure, the process, and the outcome (Longest 1977; Rohrbaugh 1980).

The concern for structure means that the organization evaluates the facilities within which the service is provided. The physical facilities are important because service realities are shaped by tangible things that consumers can compare with their senses (Shostack 1977). The ambience of a restaurant, for example, will signal to the consumer the kind of service he or she can expect. In other words, the consumer places much reliance on peripheral tangible clues as indicators of the intangible service being sought.

Structure also has to do with the way the personnel are organized— that is, the extent to which flexibility is afforded employees in interactions with clients/customers where much uncertainty surrounds the service outcome. It involves the extent to which rules and regulations are established to deal efficiently and effectively with clients'/ customers' problems requiring routine decisions so that the service can be dispensed with speed, timeliness, and courtesy.

The second concern around the effectiveness or quality issue involves the process. Here the focus is on the interaction between the service provider and the client/customer, including what is being done and what is not being done for the client/customer—in other words, the extent to which the service provider is meeting the stipulations and expectations of the contract. Of further import is the interdependence between the transmission of technical skills and service orientation skills to clients/customers by the service provider.

The third aspect of service quality is the outcome. Here the concern centers around the consequences of the services delivered. For example, is the patient recovering because of the services of the health care provider? Are students gainfully employed after graduation from the educational institutions? Outcome entails a means-and-ends emphasis. It is crucial for the organization to engage in goal setting and planning for the final outcome.

THE GOAL ATTAINMENT APPROACH TO QUALITY

An important element in the determination of service organization effectiveness is the achievement of goals. Within this context, the effectiveness of the service is a function of how it achieves or adheres to prescribed goals or objectives.

The task objectives of the service organization have to be specified. Such concrete objectives can be in the form of purchase orders placed, pot holes filled, cases supervised, calls responded to, passenger miles recorded, and so on. The extent to which specification can be effectively done will be determined by the specific market segment of the service organization. This is because the market niche will dictate the kinds of goals, the organization characteristics, and the effectiveness criteria. To determine final outcome, then, the service organization will have to identify concrete units of services that can be counted, that are relatively homogeneous over some time period, and that display some flexibility to afford adjustment for quality changes within the market segment (Mark 1981).

SUMMARY

Quality is an important issue for the service manager because of its direct impact on the performance of the organization. The intangible characteristic of service output gives rise to potential for opportunistic behavior, which may take the form of moral hazard and adverse selection. Opportunistic behaviors make it difficult to control the quality in service production. Clients and customers may assist in the improvement of the quality of service output by monitoring, where possible, the activities of the service provider.

Service organizations may improve the quality of their output through various bonding activities that build the reputation of the organization or engender more fastidious selection of clients and customers. It is important for the organization to control the behavior of its employees who interact directly with clients and customers. These participants reflect the climate or attitude of the organization, which in turn has a direct bearing on the quality of the service as perceived by the client/customer.

9 CONTROLLING CLIENT/CUSTOMER PERFORMANCE THROUGH THE SOCIALIZATION PROCESS

One of the paramount contentions of this book is that clients/customers are members of service organizations and are crucial to the effectiveness with which organizations perform. Clients/customers may be viewed as "partial" employees (Mills, Chase, and Margulies 1983). By this we mean that they are temporary participants, and the organization must develop mechanisms as it would for any permanent employee in order to be assured that clients/customers act appropriately within the service operations. This chapter will examine some of these mechanisms, especially the socialization process.

PRODUCTIVE CLIENT/CUSTOMER BEHAVIORS

Although there is considerable variation in the types of client behaviors that facilitate productivity, several factors are common to these behaviors. The task of creating a service requires careful coordination between the client/customer and the service provider. On the basis of information provided by the client/customer, the employee applies the service technology to solve problems. Service delivery systems, especially high client contact ones, require clients to conform to a number of behavioral standards that enable the system to function smoothly and efficiently. Clients facilitate the productivity of the service organization by cooperating with the service employee, be it a psychologist, bus driver, or service station attendant. This involves behaviors that extend from the input side of the service transformation system through the system itself to the output side of the system.

Input Considerations

Clients can perform several consumption task activities even before they enter the service system itself. They can plan for the necessary encounters with the service employee. Clients of tax accountants are encouraged to bring their records with them and come prepared to ask specific questions about particular deductions. Retail customers are expected to bring their receipts with them when they return unwanted merchandise. People who change dentists can arrange for their records to be forwarded.

Client preparation may also include efforts to acquire some of the knowledge used in creating the service. This has the effect of making task coordination more collegial and potentially more efficient. Sick people can consult reference books to prediagnose their ailments, and car owners can take auto mechanics courses to assist them in interaction with repair people. When the knowledge difference between client and service provider is large, however, the range of potential conflicts is wider because the service provider is often better informed about the customer's needs and has more or better information than the customer. When the customer observes the provider's actions—for example, the tests and treatments a physician undertakes—he or she is unable to determine which one is appropriate for his or her medical needs (Holstrom 1982). Since quality and quantity of services cannot be accurately verified, when there is little disparity in knowledge between the seller and the consumer about a service issue (as in the case when a doctor becomes the patient), care is more subject to interpretation. Such decentralization of power and prestige tends to foster an environment of conflict where disagreement is open and frequent (Corwin 1969). On the other hand, there are some cases when a little knowledge is a dangerous thing, for it might lead to a commitment to self-help (Gartner and Reissman 1977) when it is unwarranted or even dangerous.

In contrast, however, there are many instances when an informed client is in a much better position to assist the service employee, as in the case of a medical examination. Here, the more symptoms the client provides for the service employee, the more accurate the diagnosis. Such assistance reduces the time factor and thus the cost of providing the service. So, while it is difficult to generalize about just what level of client knowledge is desirable, some level may be optimal for consumption task activities.

Throughput Considerations

One of the requirements of the client as a salient part of the service workflow is accurate information about the nature of the problem. This is because, as Duncan (1972) observes, the more accurate the information, the easier it is to process. Without accurate information, misdiagnosis of the problem and dissatisfaction with the adequacy of the service produced can occur.

Clients are also required not only to provide the information raw material but also to process information by choosing among alternatives. This suggests that technical cooperation by the client is an integral part of the throughput process in service organizations.

Output Considerations

Often activities are required of clients after they have departed the workflow, that is, outside the direct, personal, face-to-face contact with the service employee. Postoperative exercises may be required of the patient, and homework may be required of the student. These activities are necessary for the service to be completed to the satisfaction of the participants.

In sum, the transformation system of service organizations makes claims on clients as direct participants. And although the client may not be involved in all three subsystems—input, throughput, and output—rarely can a client escape performing some activities in at least one of the subsystems. Further, the degree of client/customer involvement within service operations may vary across organizations.

SOCIALIZING CLIENTS AS PARTIAL EMPLOYEES

Potentially, client behavior constitutes a source of uncertainty in the service organization. Clients are expected to conform to certain role requirements in order to reduce this uncertainty and thereby to protect or buffer the organization's technical core. Requiring conformity to expected roles increases the potential for predictability in the service operations and reduces the threatening aspects of the client's involvement.

One way of securing client/customer conformity is through socialization. This is a process by which organization members learn the required behavior, values, and supportive attitudes that are necessary to participate as members (Brim 1966; Van Maanen 1975)—in particular, consumer processes through which individuals learn skills, knowledge, and attitudes relevant to their functioning within the service operations as consumers of the service output. Client/customer socialization differs from full-time employees' socialization by focusing on marketplace transactions. Further, socialization of clients entails the acquisition of skills, knowledge, and attitudes necessary to production behavior, which is the enactment of the consumer's role within the organization.

Since service organizations make demands upon the consumer in the acquisition of goods and services, appropriate role behaviors are required within the service operation (Solomon et al. 1985). There are three fundamental phases to the socialization of consumers within organizations: prearrival, encounter, and change and acquisition (Schein 1968).

The Anticipatory Phase

During the prearrival or anticipatory phase, the client develops an image of what is to be experienced and comes to the service organization with a preexisting set of values, attitudes, and expectations (Merton 1957). Such predispositions may have emerged from information acquired from varied sources including other clients, friends, relatives, and the media. The work of McNeal (1964) suggests that client/customer role activities are learned through observation, participation, or initiation. Consumers learn at very young ages the activities inherent in "the shopping process" by accompanying and observing parents on shopping trips. Often as young adults, teenagers are allowed to make purchases in retail outlets, see a physician, or transact with a bank, usually under the supervision of a parent or other adults. It is through such "participation" that a significant part of the early learning of consumption roles occurs. Thus, the client arrives at the organization with a perceptual picture about the services the organization has to offer and the role he or she has to perform in the production and consumption of such service outputs.

The Encounter Phase

The second phase of the client socialization is the encounter in which the client's values, attitudes, and behavioral predisposition come into contact with those of the firm and are subjected to a series of reinforcement policies designed to encourage desired behaviors and attitudes and discourage undesirable ones. For example, clients may be expected to keep appointment schedules, adhere to queuing rules in the workflow, do homework, prepare documents, and so on. When such behaviors are displayed the organization will respond in a fashion that the client perceives as positive. Conversely, when inappropriate behaviors are displayed by the client the organization will either ignore them or react in such a manner that the client interprets the reaction as punishment (Schein 1968). Friedson (1970) has observed that priorities and expectations of employees and their clients are inherently conflictive. This observation is meaningful only when the consumer anticipatory socialization was inaccurate, that is, when the client had failed to acquire the required consumption behavior and attitudes to perform within the service operation.

When there is inaccurate anticipatory consumer socialization, the predisposed consumption skills and attitudes will come into direct confrontation with those required by the service organization at the encounter phase. The potential for such conflicts during this phase of the socialization process will vary across service organizations. Inaccurate anticipatory socialization is less likely to occur in maintenance-interactive service organizations (e.g., retail operations or banks) because of the relatively simple consumptive task activities required and the many opportunities for the consumer to acquire these skills by observing and imitating others prior to interacting with the organization. Conversely, inaccurate anticipatory consumer socialization is more likely in task- and personal-interactive services (e.g., schools, legal, medical) because of the uncertainty surrounding the required consumption activities and the relative lack of opportunities to observe and initiate such activities.

The Acquisition Phase

Having been exposed to experience in the encounter phase of the socialization process, the client/customer gravitates toward an acquisition phase or metamorphosis in which he or she develops modified ideas and behaviors (Schein 1968). The role changes that occur during this stage are often accompanied by changes in status. As the client takes on a set of tasks within the service operations, he or she moves across what Schein (1968) refers to as the organization's functional boundaries. The client takes a position within the hierarchy that may entail being a subordinate to the full-time service employee (student-teacher, patient-nurse) or even sometimes adopting a supervisory position in relation to other clients (trustees in a penal institution).

The change and acquisition phase of the consumer socialization process entails the modification of the customer's behavior and ideas in the direction deemed appropriate by the organization. It was earlier noted that the delivery system of services entails a direct personal contact by the service employee with the client/customer. Such a one-on-one relationship, as Van Maanen (1975) observes, leads generally to a powerful value-oriented socialization program, which brings about change and modification in people's behavior. Consequently, it is essentially within this transaction that the client newcomer experiences a metamorphosis and becomes a temporary insider as ne or she is given responsibility and autonomy in order to develop the necessary production skills, knowledge, and attitudes.

Although consumer socialization directly affects the overall stability of the organization, the process specifically attempts to achieve the following outcomes: (1) to have clients carry out role assignments dependably, (2) to have the clients remain with the organization, and (3) to innovate and cooperate spontaneously in achieving the organizational objectives that go beyond role specification (Katz 1964). We will examine these outcomes as they pertain to the client's association with the different types of service organizations outlined in Chapter 2.

THE SOCIALIZATION OF CLIENT ACTIVITIES

Before people can learn their expected role activities and perform adequately within organizations, they must have the ability to do so (Dunnette 1966). It is for this reason that many service organizations maintain efficiency by restricting membership to qualified clients. Schools do not admit unqualified applicants, and wholesalers refuse service to customers who are unable to resell. The skill development aspect of the client socialization process is likely to be retarded if unreliable or invalid selection devices are used in choosing clients (Feldman 1981).

Clients are solicited for their abilities or attributes that are congruent with the expected consumer task requirements and with the fulfillment of meeting the organization's goal of supplying appropriate service for consumption. Consequently, the client is able to perform several tasks that will enable the system to attain desired levels of productivity.

The amount of effort directed at client/customer selection may vary across various types of service organizations. The more complex the production-related skills and knowledge required of the client/customer, the more effort will be directed at the selection of clients with ability to perform within the service organization. In maintenance-interactive service organizations the consumption production task activities required of the client/customer are of a relatively simple nature and can readily be standardized so that there is an appeal to a wide market segment capable of performing such activities. Conversely, personal-interactive service organizations require relatively complex skills of clients, and the uncertainty inherent in such consumption production activities does not lend itself to a wide array of consumers. Thus, these organizations will direct relatively more effort at selecting clients capable of performing within their operations.

It is clear that the selection of customers may entail other criteria than the ability to perform direct production activities. Organizations may select clients on the basis of the image they are attempting to project. We have focused on the consumption task activities because of their direct association to the service operations.

DEFINING THE CLIENT'S ROLE

Adequate performance by an individual occupying a new role is largely dependent on an understanding of what others within the role set expect (Brim 1966; Katz and Kahn 1978). Newcomers are confronted with ambiguous organizational contexts and seek to make sense out of these situations. One of the principal activities in the encounter phase of socialization is clarifying the role of clients and customers. In other words, based on the reciprocal exchange of information, an attempt will be made to reduce the disparity between the client's perception of the context and the perception of the service provider.

We will examine two fundamental role behaviors that are consistent with the nature of service encounters. The first is "pivotal," which are role behaviors considered by the organization to be so vital that if the participant fails to adopt them he or she would not be considered a minimally adequate performer (e.g., timely attendance by clients, students doing their homework before class meeting). The second is "peripheral." These are behaviors that the organization considers desirable but not absolutely necessary (e.g., an airline customer making favorable remarks about the airline to other passengers).

The specific kinds of pivotal role activities for the client will depend on the type of service organization. Such consumption role definition is more problematical for clients of task-interactive and personal-interactive service organizations. Within these organizations it is difficult to capture specifically what a service output is, as such output often entails a bundle of inseparable services, resulting in uncertainty surrounding the production of the intended service output. The presence of such uncertainty implies that it is indeed difficult to discriminate between intended and unintended effects since there is a general unavailability of knowledge of cause-effect relations in how these services are produced. Consequently, client/customer roles can be enacted in task- and personal-interactive service organizations in tremendously different ways without the imposition of restrictions. Such variety in role behaviors is possible because within the context of these organizations, clients tend to acquire a repertoire of consumption skills and knowledge in response to ambiguous contexts as a result of previous exposure and learning.

In maintenance-interactive service organizations there is less difficulty in teasing out the specific pivotal roles because there is less equivocality surrounding the nature of the service output from these organizations. The bank customer fills out a deposit slip; the fast food customer reads the menu and articulates the order to the clerk. These consumption activities are fairly direct in their cause-effect relations.

KEEPING CLIENTS ATTACHED
TO THE ORGANIZATION

Service organizations allocate a lot of their resources to the building of client/customer loyalty. When new clients leave the organization before the service is complete, the organization has failed to transform these outsiders into active members. One of the purposes of socialization is to retain the organization's participants.

One of the attitudes clients will display before withdrawing from service organizations is dissatisfaction with the service being rendered and the roles they have to perform in the production of such service. Unwanted client withdrawal or turnover, then, will occur when there is little satisfaction with the consumption production role activities surrounding the purchase of the actual service.

A primary reason for client/customer dissatisfaction and withdrawal from the service firm is due to a disparity in expectations. Socialization will be more effective in reducing undesired client turnover when there is a congruence between the services the organization has to offer and the clientele it attempts to attract (George, Weinberger, and Kelly 1985). This is reciprocating. The clientele must also seek congruence between the services desired and the organization that provides them.

Consumer socialization processes work through subtle interpersonal mechanisms, namely observation and imitation (Ward and Wackman 1973). This means that the potential for a match between the required production-related skills and the clientele capable of performing such skills will vary across service organizations. Maintenance-interactive service organizations require consumer skills that are relatively simple and homogeneous. For example, filling out a deposit slip for one bank is much like filling one out for another bank, and the shopping skills for retail stores will not vary greatly. Further, there is more opportunity to observe and imitate the production-related skills, knowledge, and attitudes in order to perform within these service organizations. Anticipatory socialization will tend to be generally accurate. Consequently, there will be a greater probability of congruence between the production role requirement of the service organization and the customer's expectations.

The direct skills, knowledge, and attitudes relevant to production behavior in task- and personal-interactive service organizations entail an element of uncertainty and are thus more heterogeneous. Consumer role requirements will tend to vary not only across organizations but even for each contact episode within the transaction. Further, the required production role activities for these services are difficult to learn through observation and imitation because of their complexity and the general infrequency with which people come into contact with these organizations. There is therefore a greater probability for inaccurate anticipatory socialization, resulting in an incongruence between the services desired and the organization's consumer role requirement. Much of this kind of incongruence is actualized in a direct confrontation at the encounter phase of the socialization process.

It seems clear that clients can develop an inaccurate perception of what is required of them in service operations. When service organizations fail to portray accurately both the kinds of services they have to offer and the client's role in the production of such services, there is a strong likelihood that clients will be brought into the workflow where they (1) will be exposed to services that are incongruent with their needs and (2) will be assigned roles for which they are ill prepared. As a consequence of these factors, clients will display dissatisfaction with the services they are asked to consume. Conversely, when there is a fit between the clients' abilities and the required task activities and adequate client preparation, satisfaction with the service output will increase. Further, once the clients expend effort and time in learning the skills required, they develop fealty to the organization. This is at least partly because they would rather not repeat such a learning process with another organization.

The singular point here is that there must be a realistic preview of the services the organization is capable of offering and the tasks the client has to perform. When customers with inflated or unrealistic expectations join service organizations, it is reasonable to assume that their expectations will go largely unmet. These unfulfilled desires can adversely affect the customers' tenure within organizations (Wanous 1973). There is some evidence to support the proposition that when customers discover that the service being offered and their role in the generation of that service are not what they believed they would be, they are likely to change organizations. The work of Schneider and his colleagues has demonstrated, for instance, that bank customers readily change banks because of dissatisfaction with perceived climate or attitude of the organization directly projected to them by the employees (Schneider 1973; Schneider et al. 1980).

As the socialization process attempts to keep valued participants attached to the organization, it simultaneously tries to eliminate undesirable elements. Turnover may serve as a means of getting rid of questionable participants. Consequently, the socialization process may also serve to keep customers out of the operations the needs and skills of whom are incongruent with those of the organization. Such screening will occur at the encounter stage of the socialization process when the skills, values, similarities, and interests of the client and those of the service employees come into direct contact.

CUSTOMER TENURE THROUGH
WORK GROUP SOCIALIZATION

The employee work group is a major influence in the consumer socialization process. Service providers affect the client's tenure with the organization by acting as sources of reference. A reference serves largely "to orient the actor in a certain course of action or attitude" (Kemper 1968: 32). Work group references are more influential in task- and personal-interactive service organizations where required consumption skills, knowledge, and attitudes tend to be of a more ambiguous nature. Within this context clients/customers are exposed to a set of significant others as a prime factor in the influence of attitudes and skills. But such influence is more effective when there is consistency in the expected production role cues.

Cue consistency means that there is little difference in the relevant production skills, knowledge, and attitudes for consumption behavior among significant others, that is, those service providers whom the client considers to possess important information and have credibility. Thus the service employees in direct contact with the client must set the framework with internal similarities or cues for that client so that appropriate behaviors may be developed. In essence, guidelines are being established by the service organization through the full-time service employees for making some judgment about problematic issues faced by clients. Guidelines provide a mechanism for the newcomer to identify the pivotal role behaviors so crucial to performance within the service operations. Thus, by specifying the required organization consumption context—that is, with what group or individual the customer will interact and the consistency of cues within this framework—the consumer newcomer is molded into providing appropriate kinds of behavior and information necessary to provide the service.

Service employees and work groups can affect client socialization and tenure with the firm by controlling the information flow to the client. An employee "can filter out information that contradicts dominant values, so that values may be more readily accepted by newcomers" (Feldman 1981: 314). Thus, the employee can affect not only the quality but also the amount of information raw material in the transaction with the client. Since an essential element of any role a newcomer takes on is knowledge, then by controlling the information flow to the client the employee is capable of directly affecting the client's satisfaction with the service outcome being sought and the individual's intention to remain with the organization.

Although information exchange is utterly crucial in the reciprocal interdependence between the service employee and the client, the extent to which information is meaningfully transmitted is a function of the client's perception of the employee. People employ interpretation schemes that are developed by experience or through their exposure to other situations. Consequently, misinterpretation or inappropriate interpretation may occur and can have adverse effects. Being human, clients are reactive raw materials. They often have preconceived notions as to how the service should be performed or may attribute permanence to a relatively temporary association with an organization (e.g., a patient's reluctance to break with his or her physician after recovery). Client newcomers confronted with such role ambiguity will look for interpretive mechanisms that will clarify the expectations of others and in so doing make their behaviors more consistent with such expectations.

Affecting the client's receptivity is their confidence in the information being received. Indeed, the socialization of the client is largely dependent on how much trust he or she has in the service employee. If the client perceives the employee as being a credible (that is, competent, successful, trustworthy) source of information, then he or she will be more likely to be receptive to the influence of that employee.

The perception of employee credibility persuasion may vary across service organizations. The production role activities required of maintenance-interactive service organizations are of a relatively simple, unequivocal nature. Client receptivity can be enhanced when the full-time service employee and client are similar in economic, social, physical, and personality characteristics.

The bases for credibility persuasion in task- and personal-interactive service organizations may be quite different. Within the operations of these organizations, the consumer role activities are relatively imprecise and more subject to interpretation. Thus, customer receptivity will be enhanced when there is a disparity in perceived knowledge and prestige between the service employee and customer. Similarity in the knowledge, economic, social, physical, and personality characteristics between customer and service employee in these organizations results in the equalization of power and prestige, which will further tend to generate conflict as frequent disagreement will emerge (Corwin 1969).

A typical response to enhance credibility persuasion within task- and personal-interactive services is to place social distance between the client and the service provider and to mystify the service technology. Yet, these distancing efforts may serve in some cases to interfere with the ability of the service organization to keep clients.

Without confidence in the source of information, the consumer will not be able to learn the skills, knowledge, and value system appropriate to function as a partial member within the organization. But the perception and response of the client to organization information is not solely dependent on the credibility of the employee in the interaction. Such perception and response, especially in ambiguous consumption task-related activities, is complicated by individual differences. It is therefore to be expected that the particular attributes of clients may affect the learning process.

SOCIALIZING THE CLIENTS TO INNOVATE AND COOPERATE

Organizations cannot depend solely on rules and regulations to ensure effective performance of their participants. It is primarily for this reason that Katz (1964) points out the necessity for organizations to foster an environment for innovative and relatively spontaneous supportive behaviors. The encouragement of this sort of client action has special meaning within many service contexts. In task- and personal-interactive service organizations the quality of service output cannot be easily verified, which renders the enforcement of standards problematical. Thus, solutions to issues can indeed emerge from varied sources—a fact that is consistent with the need to role make within this context. It is, therefore, in the interest of these types of organizations to encourage innovative actions among their clients and other participants. And it is largely through the socialization process that the individual learns the value of such actions to the overall effectiveness of the organization. Conversely, greater client/customer involvement and innovation may not be desired by maintenance-interactive service organizations in the interest of predictability and standardization of consumption-related procedures. Instead, consumers are encouraged simply to conform to specific direct skills, attitudes, and norms.

Essentially, in order to encourage innovative and spontaneous actions in task- and personal-interactive service organizations there is an attempt to develop what Schein refers to as "creative individualism" (1968). This means that the client will accept the pivotal or absolutely essential consumer role activities, norms, or values but reject many of the relevant or peripheral ones. For example, students will attend classes and do their homework assignments but do not necessarily participate in extracurricular activities. Patients must keep appointments and follow the prescriptions of the physician but are not required to promote the medical practices of the hospital or seek a second opinion. Creative individualism recognizes that every role has a certain minimum standard or requirement regarding adequacy of performance. Although such adequacy is virtually a condition for receiving the minimum rewards contingent on consumer role performance within the organization, it is possible for the individual to innovate outside these pivotal requirements through the expansion of the consumer role activities.

Role expansion will be accompanied by a certain number of privileges to be enjoyed by the individual consumer in the production of the service. Such privileges, as Sieber (1974) argues, serve largely as inducements and enabling mechanisms because they afford the individual a free hand in specific role behaviors. In accordance, the role expansion or job enlargement of the client will also entail freedom of the individual to act, and liberties are instrumental in innovative performance.

The increase of other roles outside the pivotal production role activities is a form of role inflation, an expansion of one's "freedom of action without recourse to formal authorization" (Sieber 1974: 572). Patients, for example, may actually monitor certain symptoms beyond what is necessary; college students may organize study groups; plaintiffs may research precedents for the defense of their position; retail customers may move hazardous obstacles out of the aisle. As such, additional rights or liberties are allotted to the consumer without accompanying formal obligations. It is largely through this process that the organization benefits by the infusion of new ideas from the client and more effective modes of providing the service to the consumer.

Production innovative behaviors can also be encouraged by allowing the consumer to experience some success through the linking of rewards to performance with the service operations. Feldman (1981) found that students who experienced initial academic success were more likely to interact with faculty members outside of class and become involved in research projects and extracurricular activities. Thus, by directly making rewards contingent on performance, the organization fosters an environment in which the client can develop the skills necessary for innovative activities. This process of growth may be tempered by the newcomer's individual consumer differences. For instance, students with high self-esteem or high self-perceived competence are more likely to expand their role activities than students with low self-esteem.

DECOUPLING THE CLIENT FROM
THE SERVICE SYSTEM

Just as clients have to be socialized into appropriate role behaviors, so must they be removed from such roles upon the completion of the service. Patients often remain attached to physicians long after they really need to; the number of years it takes some students to matriculate from college well exceeds acceptable limits; patrons linger in restaurants too long. Consequently, it is necessary for the organization to signal to its clients when their activities are no longer needed. This is a form of decoupling (Meyer and Rowan, 1977).

But such decoupling of clients from the service transformation system may pose difficulties for the organization. In maintenance-interactive service organizations where the consumer role activities are relatively simple and specific, it is possible to determine, to a significant degree, the expected output and when such output is completed. Consequently, customer withdrawal from the operations is voluntary and entails little complication. This is not the case for task- and personal-interactive service organizations where there is a potential for clients to linger in the operations. There are two main reasons for this. One is, of course, the uncertainty surrounding the output of these service organizations and the complication of exogeneous factors involved with their outcomes. Such uncertainty may pose hidden risk to the clients as the service outcome may preclude action. For example, health care patients may remain in a hospital for fear of unknown consequences that could emerge from the care they received. Such preoccupation may lead to an inability to act in ways that would help prevent such feared consequences. Within this high uncertainty context, cause-effect relations are not readily established. It is therefore generally difficult to determine when services and the accompanying role activities performed by the client in the generation of such services should cease.

Client decoupling is also problematical because it is potentially unsettling to both the organization and its clientele. From the perspective of the task- and personal-interactive service firm, clients have an ambivalent association with the organization. In one respect, these clients have to be removed from the service operation and their roles curtailed when the organization feels that the service is complete. On the other hand, such curtailment is a risky process because the organization may, and indeed generally does, desire the client's future involvement should the individual require services at a later date. For the organization, then, the client has to be removed from the transformation system upon completion of the service but must still be somewhat affiliated with the organization. In other words, the client should no longer be "in" the system but only "attached" to it. It is in this transition from active temporary member to affiliate that the potential for client alienation resides.

The decoupling of clients' role activities by signaling to these individuals when the service is complete can be accomplished in several ways. Design contracts may be established, which often place an appropriate time constraint on the service. This will also signal to the client how long his or her role activities will be needed within that service operation. The client can then be prepared for his or her removal. Physicians often prepare patients as the time for being discharged approaches by assuring them that they are getting well. It is also not unusual to find ceremonies closely linked to the time constraint, which further serve as a process of client removal from the service operations.

When clients remain within the operation of services longer than desirable for the organization, it is possible to socialize these individuals out of the system by subjecting them to various reinforcement procedures. Such reinforcement procedures may take the form of simply ignoring the client's activities or giving feedback that is perceived as punishment by the client.

SUMMARY

Consumers of services have important role activities to perform in the production of the service output. As active participants, consumers have to acquire the knowledge, skills, and disposition that will enable them to perform as effective, though temporary, members of service organizations. For some consumer activities, rules can be established that control such behaviors. Generally, clients/customers will have to be socialized into the required role behaviors. Clients/customers can be made more productive participants when there is a match between the required production-related skills, knowledge, and attitudes and the abilities and attitudes of the client/customer. This can be accomplished, to some degree, during the anticipatory socialization phase in which effort can be directed at selecting and preparing consumers for the expected production activities. The socialization process may be employed to stimulate client innovation where such behavior is warranted, especially in complex service operations.

Service organizations can reduce consumer turnover and realize productivity gains when the boundary between their employees and clients/customers is reduced. This will enable the organization to establish socialization mechanisms that would prepare both the consumer and the service provider to become better participants within the operations.

10 ORGANIZING PROFESSIONALS

One of the most rapidly expanding segments of the service sector is professional labor. This segment has shown a growth rate of 5.1 percent per annum relative to 2 percent growth for the overall labor force (Stanback et al. 1981). Especially noteworthy about the expanding professional labor force is that more of these people are moving away from the tradition of working as individual proprietors. Instead, most professionals (e.g., medical, legal, engineering, consulting, public accounting, financial) are now organizing themselves into group practices or more complex structures. Very little has been documented about the governance of these organizations.

This chapter will examine the design of professional organizations. Before proceeding with this analysis it is in order to point out the salient features of what we view as professionals. We will adopt the perspective that the designation of a person as a professional is essentially a symbolic and honorific status conferred on a person deemed to be competent in a specific body of knowledge and skill that requires prolonged specialized training. By acquiring this knowledge and the status that accompanies it, the professional has the right or social authority not only to determine problems but also to apply the appropriate solutions.

To a significant degree, the honorific status of the professional emerges from the association among a specific group of like individuals who are also regarded as well schooled in the specific body of knowledge. Such a group constitutes what is generally referred to as a profession. Since the work performed by professionals requires a high degree of skill, knowledge, and expertise it is generally recognized that only the profession or other professionals are in a position to accurately assess the performance of the individual member. Thus, there is a tendency for the members within the profession to depend on their colleagues to control just who are the competent members (Hall 1968). For example, the American Medical Association has invented mechanisms in their policing functions for screening out those who are potentially capable of doing great damage to clients.

Professions' self-policing is crucial for the client because what professionals actually do is nebulous and uncertain and the effects are often difficult to measure. In other words, the services provided by the professional are such that an incompetent act can have severe consequences for clients. Certification signals to clients some minimum level of competence.

Another important attribute of the professional is a belief in self-responsibility, or an ethic centering around the notion that the work being done is an indispensable service to the public. The idea of self-responsibility further suggests that the professional can be relied upon to work conscientiously and with a certain amount of perceived zeal. There is thus a "service-orientation" ethic, which may take the form of doing what is in the client's best interest and not necessarily what the client wants (Blau and Scott 1962).

In most professions the members are generally allowed relatively more autonomy than that given to nonprofessionals. Many of the services offered by professional service providers are rendered on a one-to-one basis with a high degree of customization for each project or case (Maister 1983). This is largely a pooled technological integration where the professional works alone with clients although there may be some sharing of equipment, buildings, and so on. The autonomy is quite understandable when one considers the responsibility afforded the professional. Since standards are so difficult to predetermine or measure objectively, the professional service provider will be responsible for the variation in the quality of services being rendered to clients. Further, the autonomy is necessary because the service provider has to have the independence not only to define problems and generate the appropriate solutions but also to do so without pressure from parties with vested interest which may include client, customer, nonmembers of the profession, or even an employing organization. The distinction between diagnosis and execution is one of the paramount differences between the professional and the technician (Maister 1983).

The importance of professional services in the economy and the dearth of information directly pertinent to the operation of these service providers stimulated the following research in this area.

THE FLEXIFORM DESIGN

We examined twenty-one professional organizations in the task-interactive service category, which included marketing-advertising agencies, engineering consulting and research, finance, and real estate companies. Two-thirds of these professional organizations were small companies, reflecting the proliferation of small organizations among professional firms. The distinction between a small and a large organization was based on the number of full-time equivalent employees. A firm with less than 100 employees was considered small. The range in size for the organizations examined was from 20 to 1,024 full-time equivalent employees.

Interviews with upper level managers were conducted. These interviews were both open-ended and structured. Managers were asked specific and general questions about the design of their organizations and the client's involvement with these organizations. In studying these organizations it became clear that they displayed a pervasive structure that could best be described as a flexiform structure depicted in Figure 10-1.

The governance structure of professionals within the flexiform framework is fundamentally centered around power and authority within organizations. We will define power as the potential to accumulate resources by deliberately affecting the behavior of others. The primary object of power and its accumulation by organization participants is to facilitate the production function within organizations.

The flexiform structure consists of a set of concentric power circles. The model can be perceived as a three-dimensional power sphere that decreases in power as one moves toward the core but simultaneously increases in authority. For our purposes we will adopt the widely held view of authority as being a subset of power that emerges from the position one occupies in an organization. Authority is a right to make decisions for others based on one's position.

Figure 10-1. The Flexiform Model of Professional Structure.

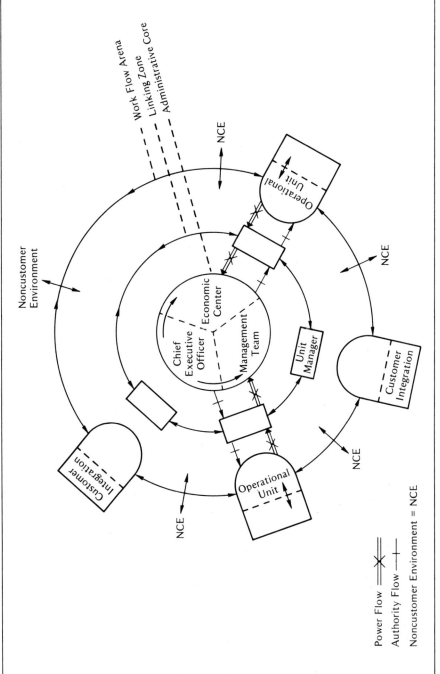

Source: Mills et al., "Flexiform: A Model for Professional Service Organizations," *Academy of Management Review* 8 (1983): 118–131.

The outer circle is the most powerful segment and constitutes the fundamental operational unit in which the client is an integral part. It is within this circle that contracts are established between the service provider and clients and where pivotal encounters are developed. There is uncertainty inherent in these encounters, as it is difficult for the service provider to specify in advance both what the client will specifically need and how to go about filling this need. The power of the service provider within this arena emerges from his or her possession of resources potentially capable of addressing the uncertainty brought by clients to the production process. This outer circle can be viewed as the primary operating core of the flexiform structure.

The second dimension of the model consists of the unit heads. Although there is relatively more authority at this level, there is less power than at the outer operating core because there is less uncertainty. The third dimension consists of the main administrative body, which may entail the management team, the chief executive officer, and the economic center. Within this context, encounters with clients will not be pivotal encounters but will be restricted to peripheral encounters or ones that are supportive to the pivotal ones (see Chapter 3 for a discussion of pivotal and peripheral encounters).

The flexiform model may easily be confused with the matrix structure. There are, however, marked differences. A matrix organization design is essentially a combination of two different structures, one functional and the other project. The functional or line organization provides a pool of experts who spend part of their work time on temporary projects that may come up. Upon completion of the project, these individuals return full time to their functional positions or homes. The matrix is a blend between the traditional hierarchical organizational form and a less rigid project form. It is an evolutionary form that attempts to focus resources on specific targets for limited periods of time. Within the matrix the functional segment and the project segment are tightly interdependent, even indispensable, to the functioning of each other (Cleland 1969). In a sense, the association between the project and functional segments is symbiotic because they are different subsystems that complement one another.

In the flexiform model there is a clear reduction in the dependence on the functional or line segment. The flexiform structure is more like a pure project organization in which there are many projects occurring simultaneously. Unlike the matrix, the flexiform does not remain saddled to some hierarchical segment that would inhibit the organization's ability to respond and adapt to a dynamic, unpredictable external environment. Ansoff and Brandenberg's (1971) idea of the innovative structure—a temporary form that has a built-in mechanism for taking project ideas directly to the marketplace—is very reflective of the flexiform model.

The flexiform, as the name suggests, varies in design, which is primarily dictated by the vicissitudes of the environment, particularly the client uncertainties. If traditional organization structures are restrictions on reality, then the object of the flexiform model is to reduce such restrictions in uncertain environments. The model is a means by which management deals with the copious amounts of information present in an uncertain environment. In stable environments, especially ones that are not very complex, the service needs of clients/customers can be readily predicted and specific or complete contracts established between the service provider and the client/customer. The governance or control of these service organizations and much of the crucial information they need can be readily processed at the strategic apex of the organization. Within these organizations the decisionmaking process can be segmented, decision management (decision initiation and implementation) being delegated to the lower levels and decision control (ratification and inspection) restricted to the upper levels. The traditional hierarchical structure is most appropriate for such relatively stable environments. When the environment becomes complex and unstable there is likely to be information overload at the top if the hierarchical structure is employed. Consequently, the reasonable solution is to decentralize decisionmaking by not segmenting this process at the primary operating core. This will loosen the rigid structure into a more flexible one in order to better adapt to environmental uncertainties.

FUNCTIONAL POWER AND AUTHORITY IN THE MODEL

Power and authority are two separate mechanisms important to the effectiveness of the flexiform model. It is necessary to delineate them clearly. Dubin (1958) views authority as the domain of an individual within an organization who has the right to make decisions for others in situations in which alternatives exist. Authority is significant to organizational interactions because it establishes the legiti-

Figure 10-2. Power and Authority Matrix.[a]

	Authority	Power
Decisionmaking Behavior	1. Affects Others	2. Affects Self
	3. Affects Self	4. Affects Others

a. Derived from discussions with Robert Dubin.

macy of choices for action through a superior-subordinate relationship. Authority evolves in relations between or among organization members in order to stabilize the decisionmaking process.

Functional power emerges through the activities or roles performed by members and the indispensability of these activities to the operations. Roles are prescribed activities that assign the employee a set of functions within the organization and are necessary to maintain the system in all of its states (Dubin 1963). With high workflow uncertainty, high task uncertainty, and the reciprocal interdependence between the professional and the client, professionals become indispensable in their boundary-spanning capacity. Within this context it is possible to examine the relationship between the notions of authority and functional power as shown in Figure 10-2.

The figure shows that authority, as earlier noted, is making decisions for others, and functional power is making decisions for oneself. The professional may make decisions that affect others (authority) and self-interest decisions (power).

The power-authority dichotomy is sharply delineated in the flexiform model. There is much authority and limited power at the administrative level. The converse would be expected at the operational level, where relatively more power and less authority exists.

In Chapter 5 we adopted the view of power as the ability to accumulate resources by having others behave in a desired way. There are two basic forms of power: active and potential. Potential power is power at rest. It is the ability to bring into the interaction resources that did not exist before. Active power is the actual bringing of such resources into a power relationship.

In cell 3, for example, a lawyer may solicit information from clients and in so doing essentially gather data for himself or herself because of the authority to secure such information. The lawyer's position (authority) gives him or her the right to act within this capacity. Conversely, (cell 4) in the process of exercising the right to secure the needed information raw material on which decisions will be made, clients (and other employees) are required to reciprocate by providing the necessary information primarily because of the lawyer's actions. This is a form of active power.

If the client provides the information without the active involvement of the lawyer (through the process of socialization, for example) then we would shift into cell 1. The client would now be performing within a mutually accepted position as a member of the organization with the right to do so.

The professionals within the operating units have strong power at the customer–firm interface. But such power is due to the indispensable roles they perform in the interface, especially in pivotal ones. Robert Dubin (1963) refers to these activities as power "in" a given situation. Within professional organizations the power bases are built more by functions than by people. This gives rise to a structure that is both horizontally and vertically decentralized as the decisionmaking process is forced down to the lower level participants or professionals. In other words, the access of professionals in the lower levels of the organization to crucial information from clients/customers makes it impossible to centralize the structure.

SELF-CONTAINED OPERATIONAL UNITS

Within the operating core of the flexiform structure are self-contained, relatively autonomous functional units. These units are the fundamental production segments in the organization's workflow. Each unit operates as a small company, and for the organizations we examined, the units varied in size from twelve to forty-three employees. Within each operational unit people often work in small teams the composition of which may change from situation to situation. As "mini-firms" within the primary operating core, these operating units are goal directed where some profit target is set based on the availability of resources in that unit. Here a budget serves as a governance mechanism or guideline for the unit's overall performance. Overseeing the activities of each functional unit is a unit manager.

Although autonomy is extended to each functional unit, there is a simultaneous necessity to coordinate the units because there is interunit dependence. Functional units may actually purchase services from each other when there is a need to do so. If, for example, unit A requires the services of an expert electrical engineer who happens to be a member of unit B, unit A will negotiate with unit B to purchase the engineer's services. This kind of business transaction will generally take place between the managers of the units.

The functional units are not restricted to securing resources solely from other units within the organization. Resources or services can also be acquired by functional units outside the organization. Generally, such outside resources are restricted to situations in which the "parent" organization is unable to provide resources needed by a functional unit at what the unit perceives is an economically reasonable price. Most of the outside human resources are secured from free-lance experts. The setting of targets for functional units through budgets coupled with the autonomy afforded each unit fosters a competitive internal milieu, which is perceived as beneficial to the overall performance of the organization. But such competition is tempered by the requirement that functional units must first seek actively to secure extra resources from among other units within the parent organization. Although teams within the organization tend to act in their own self-interest, there is a full awareness that their future is somewhat dependent on the survival of the organization (Fama 1980). Consequently, there is an inherent dependency among other functional units and a tendency to cooperate.

ROLE NEGOTIATION

The task activities necessary in rendering the service in pivotal professional encounters are nebulous. For this reason the service provider will have to spend much effort in "role making" and "negotiation" (Bucher and Stelling 1969). In the pivotal encounter with clients, the professional service provider will not have a clearly defined preexisting role for his or her behavior. Since there are so many possible contingencies around the task activities, the service provider will have to establish his or her own place in the organization by creating and developing a role. Managers and supervisors cannot specify the set of activities these service providers should be performing. Once the service provider has joined the service organization, his or her job duties are largely dependent on what he or she actually does in the transaction with clients. In other words, the professional service provider constructs or enacts his or her role activities and justifies these activities to the organization. This is knowledge technology where individuals have to find rationale for their activities. This notion of role creation is clearly depicted, for example, in the legal profession or consulting firms. When one lawyer (or consultant) replaces another, the new lawyer (consultant) does not take the role of his or her predecessor because they will differ in their perceptions of how the case should be handled, their interactions with clients, their competence, the manner in which they organize their activities, the pace at which they work, and so on. In other words, the professional's job becomes idiosyncratic.

Role making and negotiation are inextricably linked because the notion of role creation dictates the presence of negotiation. For the service provider, the negotiation occurs as an ongoing process in the establishment of contracts not only with clients but also with supervisors within the organization. Within the context of the flexiform organization, the professional is under contract with that organization to provide a service, which is in turn subcontracted to clients. Since the particular role activities cannot be easily contracted between the flexiform organization and the professional employee, the contracts established will necessarily be incomplete. Consequently, there will be a continuous process of negotiation and renegotiation of contracts as the professional attempts to create, develop, and modify his or her role performance in the face of changing situations.

THE FLEXIBLE FOCUS EMPLOYEES

The complexity and uncertainty surrounding much of what professionals actually do requires people with certain attributes necessary to perform in this environment. Not all employees are capable of operating in an environment in which roles are not well defined and have to be created. Employees who expect supervisors to set forth specific role prescriptions about how to perform in the encounter with clients will be out of place within the flexiform environment. Thus, one of the major goals of the functional unit of the flexiform structure is to encourage the development of what Dubin, Champoux and Porter (1975) call flexible focused employees. Within the functional unit professional employees are often required to make frequent and sometimes drastic changes from one situation to another largely in response to clients' demands. It is primarily for this reason that employees are encouraged to perform a variety of task activities. The attempt to become a flexible employee is a crucial adaptive technique that allows the individual to adjust to diverse behavioral situations by varying his or her commitment to the situation. The diversity of task activities emerges from interacting directly not only with clients but also with peers, since team effort is prevalent. Thus, the flexible focused person must possess not only complex knowledge but also an adaptive personality.

A salient spin-off from having employees that are flexible focused is creating an environment for entrepreneurs. By this we mean that there are opportunities for the employee to take risks by becoming what Simmel (1971) refers to as an adventurer. Since the professional deals with equivocal information, as an adventurer he or she attempts to reduce such equivocality by creating a system where none previously existed. In other words, the professional has to be adventurous in trying to make sense of nebulous situations.

The degree of flexibility employees are allowed is a function of the degree to which the activities being performed by the individual can be objectively assessed. Because the roles within the units tend to be largely ill defined, objective assessment cannot be readily achieved. Consequently, the employee has to be allowed much discretion. There is also a direct association between the flexibility of the employee and the amount of responsibility that employee is afforded, which will in turn reflect the extent to which the decisionmaking process is segmented. The responsibility afforded the flexible focused employee will be in direct response to the dynamics of the environment in which the professional organization finds itself, and this varies across industries. For example, in the engineering construction industry, where a tremendous amount of information is needed from clients, individual employees and the firm can be held legally responsible to the client should the decision unit incur an irresponsible error to the detriment of the client.

THE ISSUE OF MOBILITY

Unlike the case in many other organizational forms, the notion of employee upward mobility is generally not encouraged by the flexiform structure. This is due to the tendency of the flexiform structure to be relatively flat, that is, to have few levels of management. It was generally felt among managers that an ethic of promotion was unimportant to the social milieu, and as a result, there was very little vertical promotion reported. The rationale for the deemphasis on promotion is based on how the structure is perceived. Managers generally believed that the traditional bureaucratic structure presented an illusion of widespread mobility based on the belief that openings within the firm were immediately created for the subordinate when the individual had become promotable.

Mobility refers to a change in status for the individual within the functional unit. It is a movement from one general classification to another, and it entails a period of probation for the participant (Dubin 1958). All the flexiform organizations examined had probationary periods for participants after which some form of tenure was granted. In most cases, nontenured members were highly monitored. The tenure principle is basically an entitlement process because it has the potential for allowing the individual to share in net cash inflows, participate in strategic and policymaking decisions, earn a high salary, and obtain higher status (Maister 1983). Tenure will only affect the flexiform structure if the tenured employee is also elevated to the managerial ranks. The flatness of the flexiform structure tends to reduce both the expectation of upward mobility and the desire and significance of hierarchical supervisory position. This is consistent with Fama's (1980) observation that when jobs are highly idiosyncratic, the promotional ladders will tend to be thin and long, access being largely restricted to the operating core.

Within the functional unit employees are more concerned with the actual task to be performed. But the autonomy of the functional unit provides an opportunity for most individuals to become "leaders" of projects. Since projects are of relatively short duration, there is potential for members to engage repeatedly in supervisory activities by heading up different projects. This type of supervision is temporary and dependent on the kinds of activities within the functional unit. What is most important here is that the employee in the flexiform structure does not have to abandon his or her technical or operational position, peers, or even the unique values within the unit in order to engage in supervisory activities. Thus, the flexiform structure encourages and attracts people who value occupational progress within their profession rather than progress along a career path within the firm. It attracts engineers who would rather remain good engineers than become managers.

THE ECONOMIC CENTER

An important element within the flexiform structure is the economic center. This is essentially an administrative support system and consists of the general manager and the specialized economic administrations. The economic center has several fundamental functions, one of which is to take care of many of the routine activities that are perceived by the functional units as burdensome. An effort is made to pool these activities and realize some economies of scales of administration. This unit tends to be somewhat more hierarchical, as it is possible to separate the decisionmaking process, with lower level employees within this unit engaging in decision management and supervisors engaging in decision control. The economic center also serves as a crucial integrator because its activities are common and supportive to all the functional units.

The primary mechanism used to assist the economic center is the data-processing system. The data-processing system acts as an added monitor for the overall unit performance by providing statistical information about budget goals and thus fostering a kind of centralized control, although operational activities of the functional units tend to be decentralized. The functional units do not operate as pure profit centers but instead as semiprofit centers because of their heavy dependence on the economic center for their administrative activities. It is generally recognized within the flexiform model that the information-processing system is not employed in monitoring the actual task activities within the operational unit per se. This function remains within the operational unit and under the control of the unit manager. The information system within the economic center is cost effective because it tends to reduce the number of administrative staff, especially those involved in clerical activities.

THE GENERAL MANAGER OF
THE FLEXIFORM MODEL

An important element within the flexiform model is the general manager. It is the role of the general manager to pull the autonomous functional units into some cohesive whole. The general manager thus emerges as the primary integrator within the organization as an attempt is made to foster interunit interaction. One way of viewing the manager is as an individual with dual roles. On the one hand, he or she is the dominant figure in the economic center running the administrative activities, handling issues around compensation and vacations, providing information about performance, and so on. This individual is also an active part of the management team as a primary facilitator in the interunit coordination. Consequently, general managers spend some of their time as arbitrators attempting to resolve interunit conflicts.

The role of the general manager also extends into the external environment of the organization. He or she is responsible for expanding the client system and has the task of allocating clients among the functional units. This is not difficult when functional units tend to have specialties. The allocation of clients is problematic when there is little difference in interunit specialization. Within this context, functional units tend to perceive their resources as being most appropriate for rendering services to clients. The general manager has to move beyond this provincialism and provide the customer with the resources that will best meet his or her particular needs. The general manager makes an effort to stimulate technological innovation by encouraging employees to keep abreast of new developments in their fields. This will improve the organization's activities, especially at the primary operating core.

Another of the general manager's roles is to encourage a sense of cost consciousness throughout the organization. Much effort is therefore directed at activities concerning budgets or the allocation and utilization of resources. Within this context, the manager often has to balance the degree to which functional units secure needed services outside the organization with utilization of available resources within the firm. He or she must actively encourage the use of internal resources among units, and one way of fostering interunit interaction is by employing the economic center to create interunit interdependencies.

THE MANAGEMENT TEAM

A paramount governance mechanism in the flexiform structure is the management team. This control element consists of the leaders of the

Figure 10-3. Administration-Functional Unit Integration.

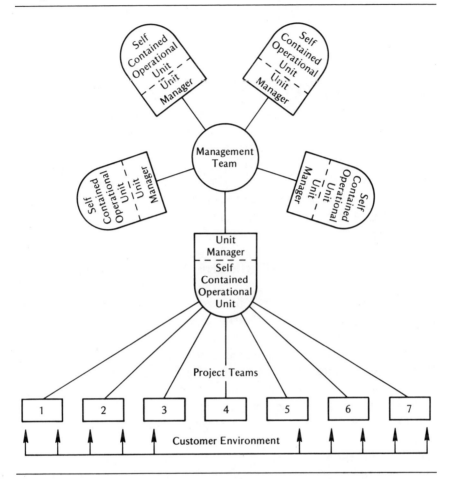

functional units and the general manager. The management team attempts to serve as a crucial link between the functional units and the economic center. The team also acts as an integrator in trying to coordinate the functional units (see Figure 10-3).

Just as important, members of the management team attempt to protect their operating cores from interruptions that may adversely affect performance. To accomplish this, the unit manager has to be perceived not only as being well informed and reliable, but more significantly as having influence with, and the respect of, the general manager.

The management team has significant influence on the overall performance of the organization. It is within this unit that standards for determining performance are established. Here, for example, it is determined whether to use a companywide standard, such as the amount of billable client hours per employee, to evaluate performance. The management team establishes the broad policies of the organization, which may include, for instance, the income distribution among the members, budgets and profit projections, and methods of soliciting clients. Since the manager of each functional or operating unit is also a member of the management team, each employee in the operating core is represented at the policymaking level of the organization. Essentially, the management team attempts to foster the internal flow of information not only horizontally through mutual adjustment but vertically as well.

SUPERVISION WITHIN THE OPERATIONAL UNIT

Professional service providers in direct encounters with clients require varying skills in both soliciting and processing the needed information. Since the decision process within the operational unit is not separated into decision management and decision control, these contact employees are required to have skills for the inspection of activities, the correction of errors, and control of the encounter. Consequently, much of the responsibility for the task activities in the generation of the service has to be delegated to the subordinate. What emerges within this context is "worker-centered responsibility" (Dubin et al. 1965).

The notion of worker-centered responsibility suggests that within the flexiform primary operating core the supervisor spends little time instructing subordinates in task-related activities. Instead, the professional service provider practices self-supervision. The essence of worker-centered responsibility is having employees take responsibility for the management and control of their task-related activities.

The primary structural problem that favors implementing worker-centered responsibility is the inability of the organization to evaluate objectively the professional's task performance. Performance is often based on an imprecise, subjective system involving a joint supervisory-subordinate consultative approach in the absence of objective standards and measurement tools. What is really occurring here is the negotiation and renegotiation of contracts. The contractual stipulations begin with and are largely dependent upon the professional service provider's ability to create his or her own role. The task activities that a professional performs can hardly be determined beforehand because there are many contingencies. Thus, what the professional actually does or happens to be doing is likely to be what he or she should be doing as far as the supervisor is concerned. It is for this reason that many flexiform organizations have adopted a hybrid management by objective approach where the professional and the formal supervisor negotiate contractual goals and jointly set forth plans.

An important feature of worker-centered responsibility is that it fosters peer or colleague control. This means that there is monitoring of the professional's activities by other professionals in the operating core. Such peer monitoring is important for several reasons. Clients are often incapable of judging the services being rendered by the professional service provider. The parties most competent to judge the professional service provider's activities are peers and colleagues who are trained within the same profession. Further, since the reputation of the profession is important, the activities of an incompetent professional service provider will tend to radiate onto other members within the organization. Thus, peer monitoring attempts to maintain a firm's good reputation. It is for this reason that many flexiform organizations have tended toward group evaluation in which input is actively sought from group members. The rationale here is that an employee's performance is better known to his or her peers than to the manager since there is more interaction among peers. It is quite possible for a professional performing high uncertainty task activities, for example, to deceive a formal supervisor because of the sporadic interaction between them. But it is highly improbable that that employee will deceive his or her peers. Clients depend on this type of monitoring as a form of bonding in establishing contracts with the service organization as discussed in Chapter 8.

Worker-centered responsibility entails the tendency for professional service providers to consult with peers, rather than with the formal supervisor, when task-related problems arise. From this perspective we find the basis for managing being shifted from a legitimate power base to the realm of the expert or information source among work peers, who are often more task competent in some areas than the individual in a legitimate position.

One of the important functions of the formal supervisor will be resolving conflicts among the participants within the primary operating core. The uncertain task environment of the flexiform organization will foster role making by the professional. Since roles have attached to them privileges, rights, responsibilities, duties, advantages, and so on, there is a tendency for role inflation. Consequently, within the operating core of the flexiform organization, members seeking to role make or expand their functions in order to get their work done will tend to generate the overlapping of role activities both among professionals and between professionals and clients. The formal supervisor will be involved in defining the zones of authority in arbitrating between parties with overlapping roles. This notion of clarifying and defining authority zones tends to be an ongoing process within the operating core of the organization.

CO-OPTING THE CLIENT

A germane feature of the flexiform structure is the extent to which it is capable of co-opting the client. Co-optation is a mechanism by which the client is absorbed into the decisionmaking process of the organization in order to avert threats to its stability or existence (Selznick 1949). When people are placed in positions of responsibility they tend to become less disruptive. The flexiform design makes the client an integral part of the functional or operational unit. No other service organization structure allows so much environmental involvement in its operations. In order to allow the client into the operation as an active participant, the boundaries that traditionally separate the organization from its environment have to be opened or extended as Figure 10-4 shows. By so doing, the organization reduces uncertainty and fosters stability.

The notion of co-optation suggests that the client is important but also quite threatening. As invaluable information sources, clients become enfranchised through the process of co-optation. By being incorporated into the operations the client becomes a temporary member of the organization and thus subject to the governing mechanisms of the organization, for example the socialization processes. To a greater degree than most other organizational forms, the flexiform structure gives the client a feeling of membership because it requires

Figure 10-4. Customer-Unit Integration.

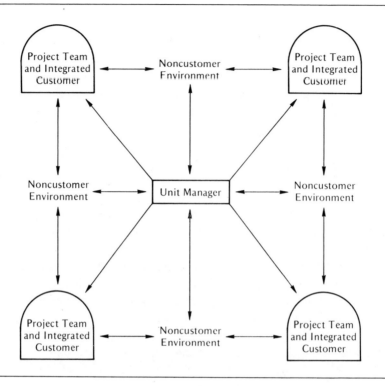

more elaborate activities of them. The client is placed in a position of status within the operational unit where he or she meets and works closely with a few people. Not only are clients required to perform in each contact episode with the service employee but, like the service employee, they are also expected to engage in preparatory activities in anticipation of the contact episode. As a result of this active involvement in the actual production of the service he or she desires, the client is co-opted into accepting some responsibility for the ultimate satisfaction of the outcome.

Client co-optation into the operations of the flexiform structure has other benefits for the organization. One advantage is that it fosters the flow of invaluable information into the service operations, resulting in better quality of service being produced. The client can also serve as a catalyst for interunit cooperation by tapping into resources from different segments of the organization.

THE DE-EVOLUTION OF FUNCTIONAL UNITS

A major problem confronting managers of the flexiform structure is a tendency for the functional units to separate from the parent organization and form new, independent organizations. Many managers reported having experienced this mitotic process, and it usually had adverse effects on the parent organization. The primary reason why such de-evolution is worrisome to managers is that the new unit invariably takes clients from the parent company. Further, the newly formed company poses a threat to the parent as a direct competitor for potential clients.

Several managers pointed out the vulnerability of the flexiform structure to the process of organizational de-evolution. There is an inherent paradox in the flexiform structure. In order for the structure to function effectively management must delegate authority to the functional units so that these units can react with autonomy to environmental uncertainty. But it is precisely this delegation of authority and the accompanying autonomy to act that create a climate conducive to separation from the parent company. The de-evolution process is also facilitated by the ease of entry into markets, relatively limited capital being required for start-up of service organizations.

Although there is a potential for the organization to lose valuable resources by being governed by a flexiform structure, the model's positive aspects make such risks worth taking. Managers have adopted many approaches in attempting to arrest the spawning of new firms from the parent. One approach is to transfer the ownership of the organization to key employees so that the firm, to some extent, becomes a worker-owned company and is very similar to the notion of partnership. From this perspective, ownership is seen as a technique for securing employee loyalty to the organization, especially among those individuals potentially capable of leaving the firm and of attracting others to leave. Of the flexiform organizations examined, such ownership was restricted to less than 20 percent of the employees. Another, more widespread approach in preventing employee flight is the bonus system or profitsharing. This approach tends to cover a relatively large number of employees.

These approaches appear to be secondary to the significance of granting authority to employees at the operating core. Managers reported that the authority dissemination approach was very important to securing employee commitment. The authority granted to the employee gives the individual the freedom to act in task-related activities. This results in the employee having a sense of participation in important decisions that affect them; thus, it generates a sense of investment of effort and serves as a subtle means of securing commitment to the organization.

SUMMARY

One of the essential features of the flexiform design is the process of role definition and redefinition by lower level professionals. This is consistent with the autonomy needed by these individuals in the face of continual negotiation and renegotiation of contracts with clients. It is therefore necessary for the decisionmaking process to be pushed to the lower levels of the organization, which increases the power of the lower participants although not necessarily their authority.

Professionals operating within this environment will have to be flexible in order to be effective. This is because systems will have to be developed where none presently exist. In such an atmosphere much of the control mechanism for the individual's performance will rely on colleague authority and self-control.

The units within the flexiform model are loosely coupled. Thus, there is a tendency for valued units and individuals to leave the organization, and this is often detrimental to the firm. It is therefore necessary for the organization to develop elaborate bonding mechanisms, such as partnerships, in order to attract, retain, and motivate such individuals.

11 THE FUTURE CRISES OF SERVICE ADMINISTRATORS

The service sector appears to be at a crucial stage in its evolution. Many areas of the sector that have been traditionally subjected to protection or regulation—for example, health care, banking, and airlines—are now being forced to operate under more competitive market conditions. Even in the public sector much attention is being directed at efficiency. Managers of services are being pressured to improve the productivity of their organizations. If managers are to realize productivity gains they must contend with two paramount concerns: issues related to the external environment and the organizing costs associated with technology.

ENVIRONMENTAL CRISES

It is clear that the performance of organizations is affected by their environment. Their behavior must reflect not only the ability to adapt to a particular market niche but more importantly the capacity to expand or find new niches for long-term survival. Adaptability requires some understanding of the environment, that is, at least being able to anticipate changes in the external environment. For managers of service organizations this is not an easy task because of the complexity of service market environments.

179

The unpredictable nature of conspicuous consumptive patterns of service consumers makes it difficult to expand and generate new market niches. Conspicuous consumption shapes the consumer's behavior. The notion of conspicuous consumption is one of pecuniary rewards and social prestige. It is an effort by the consumer to seek and to emulate. Consumers display social prestige through consumptive behavior because they possess the need for social acceptance. Thus, markets can be created or expanded by the detection of consumption trends. The ability to create markets is controlled, specifically, by the desire of people to wear, buy, and behave like others, and this desire is transmitted to a referent group through some visible or tangible cues. Thus, the extent to which the consumer engages in the detectable consumption of services is dependent on a referent group.

Conspicuous consumption is largely an expressive behavior as the consumer attempts to maintain some desired link with some other person or group. These social groups provide the consequences for the individual's consumptive act. The consumer may have several reference groups that are ordered in terms of social status and in terms of the degree to which they influence a particular consumptive situation. Within these reference groups, the consumer will directly focus on and be more influenced by significant others.

The consumer's tie to reference groups and significant others makes it possible for organizations to segment markets by developing perceived quality differences among various brands of products or kinds of services. These perceived service brand distinctions provide status symbols and further the expressive function.

Veblen (1936) formulated the notion of conspicuous consumption as an expressive behavior associated with the physical or tangible output of manufacturing organizations. Conspicuous consumption is an invidious behavior intended to stimulate like action in others. The question that arises for managers of services in their efforts to expand or develop markets is how do people conspicuously consume the output of their organizations? In other words, to what extent can the consumption of services by some consumers be emulated by others so that markets can be expanded or created?

Unlike the tangible output of manufacturing organizations, the output of service organizations is largely intangible. The status symbols that one would expect to foster expressiveness are far from apparent. The consumer's referent group or significant other does not display externally the services to be emulated. How then does the service manager expand market niches by stimulating the consumer to purchase services?

The consumer's value system toward a particular service can be segmented into two parts: expressive and utilitarian values. Utilitarian value is the consumer's desire to maximize rewards inherent in the service. This value is quite different from the expressive value, which is a person's desire to express attitudes that reflect personal values and self-concept.

The inability to display much of the service output in general creates an indispensable bond between the service consumer and the referent group or the significant other. For the service organization this means that market niches can be expanded or created by positioning, or aiming at the image of a particular referent group. The consumer has to be in a position of communicating to others the consumption of the service. Market expansion can be realized by providing consumers with the means of communicating the expressive values associated with the service. This is no easy task for the service manager. Differential advantage in terms of appealing to particular referent groups must be found. In other words, the service organization has to position itself by creating an image that will appeal to a particular referent group. And it is hoped that the consumer will be able to derive benefits from this image position by communicating to others his or her consumption of the service. But such communication is hampered drastically by the intangible nature of service consumption. The manager can realize a differential advantage by providing consumers with the means of communicating or expressing the consumption to referent groups or significant others.

There are two basic ways consumers express their consumption of a service to others. One is through personal communication in conversation with referent group members. The other is by the displaying of symbols that communicate the consumer's endorsement or consumption of a particular service (e.g., a Florida tan). Such cues may serve as the conversational interchange between the consumer and a member of his or her referent group. The difficulty for the service organization increases when no residual tangible evidence of consumption remains after the consumption of the service.

FADS AND FASHIONS IN SERVICE INNOVATIONS

The other major environmental concern for managers of services is the relative ease with which the technological innovation of one service organization can be transferred to other service organizations. Innovation means the organization bringing something new into use. This is in contradistinction to invention, which is bringing something new into being. The monopolistic position enjoyed by service innovators is generally of a very short duration, as competitors can easily adopt and produce similar services. This results in dynamic environments and thus pressure on services to innovate continuously in order to differentiate service lines. It has to be kept in mind that a service is a deed, an effort, or a performance, and what the service organization is essentially selling is its technology. This is because, as we have earlier argued, the service output cannot be separated from the activities employed in its production.

Service innovation is a function of several interdependent factors, one of which is the service provider's motivation to innovate. This is significantly affected by obstacles against innovation and the amount of resources at the disposal of the service provider to overcome or neutralize such obstacles (Mohr 1969). Obstacles to the service provider's being able to innovate may be intrinsic to the individual (e.g., limited ability, training, skills) or organization (structure, operating procedures, etc.). The primary source for the resources necessary to address these obstacles has to emerge from the organization and those responsible for its management.

Largely accountable for the ease of technological transference across service organizations are the permeable boundaries and the open system nature of services, which make it possible for the organization readily to detect changes not only from competitors but from consumers as well. Transference is further facilitated by the relative lack of capitalization of service operations, which serves to increase the flexibility of these organizations. The dynamism of most service settings creates an environment of innovative fads within the service context where changes in production techniques become ends in themselves.

Such changes are crucial in order to fulfill the service organization's "operating inventiveness" (Merton 1957) as the organization

Figure 11-1.   The Process of Innovation in Service Operations.

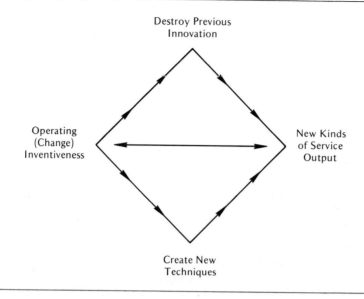

experiments with new forms and approaches to the production of the service output. This is vital for expansion and survival because it enables the organization to position itself in its market niche. Since service innovation can easily move across service boundaries, the time span for the turnover of trends in production is relatively limited.

The operating inventiveness will increase as the organization attempts to distinguish itself from competitors. As Figure 11-1 shows, operating inventiveness will eliminate previous techniques and also create new types of services. The effectiveness of operating inventiveness is dependent on the management's creating an environment conducive to such behaviors. Such an environment would entail, for example, the establishment of funds that would be set aside for innovation, and feasibility study programs. By establishing such funds, the organization creates "slack" within its operations which is primarily intended for unusual or nontraditional activities. This slack innovation is not intended for everyday or ordinary activities (Cyert and March 1963; Delbecq and Mills 1985). When such funds are unavailable or insufficient there will be a tendency for innovation to compete for resources with the existing everyday activities. This will result in a reduction in operating inventiveness. Special slack innovation funds are employed particularly when major innovations are being considered and in relatively stable markets. Here, time is relatively less critical so innovation study teams can scrutinize the new idea as it pertains to clients/customers, competitors, and even other industries.

The danger for the service organization in operating inventiveness is the temptation to engage in fad innovation. By this we mean a conspicuous adoption of innovation because it is fashionable, an attitude of change for the sake of change. In fad innovation the "means" (change) and "ends" (trends in techniques) become indistinguishable. This results in a form of innovation ritualism in which the service organization loses its mission or values because it fails to take into account the long-term consequences of the adopted innovations or techniques. This type of innovation ritualism occurs randomly as service providers adopt ideas irrespective of whether such techniques are consistent with what is in the best long-term interest of customers or the mission of the organization. In other words, there is little attempt to evaluate the effects of such service technology on the intended market niche. This type of ritualism is likely to occur when the type of technology does not require huge expenditures of capital and when there is much discretion at the disposal of the service providers in boundary-spanning positions within the organization. It is primarily through the service providers in boundary-spanning positions that innovation ritualism can sweep through the organization. These service providers act as gatekeepers linking their colleagues to crucial sources of information.

PRODUCTIVITY ISSUES

There is much debate concerning ways of improving the performance of service organizations. In order to realize productivity gains, some writers have argued strongly for the abandonment of the traditional, "humanistic" attitude and adoption of manufacturing technologies instead. The embracing of a manufacturing systems approach in the service sector, the argument posits, is to invite drastic improvement in the efficiency of the operations and the quality of the output (Levitt 1972). This means that there is a substitution of technology and systems procedures for worker discretion. The salient emphasis is on making the service operations more rational, that is, on clearly and precisely defining and carefully monitoring behaviors to ensure adherence to prescribed procedures.

There is little doubt that immense efficiency gains in the manufacturing sector have been realized through job rationalization (Roberts and Kelly 1985). And it is quite clear that service executives have begun to give serious thought to the notion of job rationalization within their organizations in attempts, for instance, at "streaming" the flow of customers and automation (employing automated teller machines—ATMs—for example). By establishing such systems the organization essentially narrows the scope of its external market in the interest of efficiency and so restricts its flexibility to respond more rapidly to change. This may be a reasonable strategy, especially for the production of simple services. However, managers have to exercise much caution in adopting such procedures because wholescale adaptation of job rationalization into their service organization will have counterproductive effects not just for the service sector but also for the larger social and economic sectors.

One of the major criticisms of the manufacturing job rationalization is its tendency to reduce workers to ersatz machines. It is well-known that costs are incurred in terms of less commitment to work and the individuals within the workplace experiencing feelings of meaninglessness and alienation. These industrial maladies may well be repeated in the service sector.

Fredrick Taylor's (1911) attempt to revolutionize workplace efficiency in the manufacturing sector around the turn of the century was met with passionate resistance from workers who complained about being reduced to mere automatons or wooden men. Such cries as "Why am I not allowed to think or move without someone interfering or doing it for me?" (p. 125) were not uncommon. In spite of Taylor's defense of this system, it may be no accident that during the period considered to be the zenith of industrial productivity in the United States industrial workers no longer found work their central life interest (Dubin 1956).

The adverse effects of work not being the central life interest entail people looking outside the workplace to engage in meaningful activity. The nature of services offers an opportunity to create a higher quality work environment. This is crucial for the service sector because, as Sassar (1976) notes, service managers have to sell their employees on what they are doing in order for these organizations to be effective. Attitudes about the organization can be transferred quite easily across boundaries and into the client interaction (Schneider and Bartlett 1970). Consequently, a decision has to be made by the service executive in terms of the nature of the service task and the efficiency of systematic techniques.

THE MAN-MACHINE RELATIONSHIP IN SERVICES

The significant factor to consider in analyzing the problem of job rationalization or the substitution of people with systematic processes is the cost consideration. This organization cost has to be evaluated in full awareness of the behavioral reactions of the employees within the organization.

Clearly, labor costs for the service organization will tend to increase in the short run because they tend to be subject to sudden spurts or fluctuations. Such fluctuations may emerge, for example, between regular time to overtime costs. When fluctuations are coupled with added costs of human necessities such as payments for worker welfare, work breaks, and so on, it is economically more attractive to set up rational systems where feasible because machines will have lower maintenance costs.

These organizing costs are essential in comparing human labor with rational or machine labor. Rational processes that include machines are faster and generally more reliable producers than is loosely organized human labor, as one would expect. However, rational processes are neutral states and become more costly when viewed in terms of the "rework" aspect of the procedure. People show superiority over machine or rational procedures where rework is necessary because of their immense flexibility in a job shop (custom) work situation or where the output has to be customized to the situation.

Rational systems attempt to establish order around activities. Such order creates stability and predictability—factors that are indispensable for efficiency because they enable the manager to plan better. A sense of order can be of much value in realizing productivity gains within organizations. Order has also spawned another kind of gain for workers by reducing the labor unit time within the production function. Thus, there is a reduction in the amount of actual time people spend in the workplace. People can therefore cultivate other life interests with the availability of more nonwork time or leisure.

The extent to which workers actually find leisure desirable is debatable. Such nonwork time as leisure is often viewed within Thorstein Veblen's (1937) definition as the nonproductive use of time.

Thus, people are saddled with the notion of leisure as a state of useless pursuits. The difficulty people experience in realizing their full potential in leisure time may be more directly and specifically related to conditioning to schedules and an inability to transcend the work discipline to which the person is so intimately bound, for most of the work activities an individual experiences are dictated by rational work systems where order and adherence to schedules are crucial. One can expect these same values to permeate the leisure domain as well. Veblen (1904) makes this point when he attributes the inability of the individual to segment work from nonwork to the discipline of rational or machine procedures in which intellectual requirements are rendered useless and therefore extinguished. Work is the dominant interest in people's existence, and it permeates all other activities in which people are engaged. How people perform their work activities is quite influencial on their nonwork activities, and attempts to increase the latter without due consideration to what is occurring in the actual work environment may be counterproductive.

CUSTOMIZING WORK ACTIVITIES

The traditional approach to productivity gains in organizations is to have people adapt as closely as possible to the nuances of rational systems. Such job rationalization is a process that, as Veblen long ago noted, "compels the adaptation of the workman to his work, rather than the adaptation of the work to the workman" (1936: 309). Although this remains the overwhelming approach to improving performance, there are some attempts to generate alternative approaches, such as the sociotechnical systems by Emery and his colleagues (Emery and Trist 1965). The essence of most of these alternative approaches is that technology should be designed to match the worker. Here attempts are being made to incorporate more fully the human element into the production function by elevating the participant to a more salient position. Thus, technology becomes secondary to the employees.

Matching the technology to the worker is extremely pertinent in service organizations where the involvement of clients/customers in the primary operating core dictates relatively more extensive activities. In other words, the production of services involves the service provider behaving in nonprescribed ways. Nonprescribed behaviors are those behaviors not required of the service provider but that he or she will choose to do because they will enhance the quality and production of the service operation. Nonprescribed behaviors are voluntary (Dubin 1956). Voluntary behaviors by the service provider are precisely the kinds of activities that are germane to the creation and expansion of market niches, and indeed such behaviors are crucial for the very survival of the service organization. This is because the subordination of technology to the employee in these services makes it possible to draw upon untapped resources. These untapped resources are essentially nonprescribed behaviors that are crucial in the generation of more complex services where much uncertainty surrounds the production of the service output. Job rationalization within this context may prove to be ineffective because it might serve to create indifference in the service provider and reduce the individual's engagement in voluntary behaviors.

There are some initial costs in the establishment of environments that encourage voluntary behaviors. Such costs may entail the risks incurred from the potential control loss. The risk of control loss emerges as responsibility and autonomy are pushed further down the organization because there is no absolute assurance of the service employee's adherence to goals and outcomes. What is gained from such risks is an approach to the service production that is potentially better able to match the client's/customer's want by reducing employee indifference and increasing voluntary behaviors. Consequently, the organization is in a better position to adapt to and expand market niches.

CONCLUSION

The transition to a service economy has created new challenges for organization theory and behavior. There is an urgency to control organizing costs, especially because of the relatively low productivity growth of service sector organizations. Novel organizing models are clearly needed to address the development of services. This book has pointed out some characteristics around which more elaborate models of the governance of well-functioning service organizations can be constructed. The book's underlying theme is that the client/customer involvement in service operations radically affects the governance of resources within these organizations. This is quite at odds with most contemporary approaches to the study of organizations. Social scientists have not been very sensitive to relationships other than employee-organization relations.

The limited application of earlier models on the control of resources in organizations to services should hardly surprise us. These earlier governance models, based largely on the notions of J. D. Thompson, were primarily anchored in and directed at manufacturing organizations. Such closed systems perspectives are meaningful for manufacturing organizations because they facilitate sealing off the technical core of these firms and as a result capitalize on the ensuing predictability of the activities. But closed systems models are questionable for service operations, in general, since the direct involvement of clients/customers in the production process makes it difficult to seal off the primary operating core. Consequently, the norms of organization rationality and closed systems notions as proposed by Thompson may not be applicable in services where there is much dependence on clients/customers and where the operations must meet market tests.

Technology is clearly important in service operations. But its relationship to control mechanisms, especially structure, is less direct than that in manufacturing firms. Technology is related to structure in low-contact services where there is little dependence on clients/customers, but it becomes weaker for those services in which there is increased contact with and dependence on clients/customers. In essence, the involvement of the client/customer in the service organization moderates the association between technology and structure. Since the client/customer is generally a crucial part of most service operations, variations in client/customer involvement would be expected to generate variations in technology.

The incorporation of the customer-firm interface or the face-to-face direct contact with the service provider as a moderator represents an improvement over earlier models on the saliency of technology in organizations. As a moderator variable, the client's/customer's involvement improves our prediction by identifying the organizations for which technology can be employed as an important predictor of structure as earlier noted. There are several implications for this fundamental model for services, including the following.

Gartner and Reissman (1974) have argued that as more workers in the future function in service roles, the boundary between employees and customers will increasingly blur. As the closeness of the customer-firm interface increases, the boundaries of the service organization (i.e., structure) are extended to allow for an active client/customer participation in production task activities.

It would seem reasonable that service managers who wish to gain a competitive advantage, especially those in high customer encounter firms, will have to design objective structures that foster entrepreneurial climates at the transformation system. Such structures should allow the service provider to fulfill boundary spanning activities such as filtering, buffering, transacting, representing, and in general protecting the service firm. As Sasser (1976) has pointed out, service employees, especially those in high-contact encounters, act as mini-firms in that they are often involved in direct production and distribution of service output simultaneously. Although many low-contact services, for example retail organizations, have begun to differentiate themselves by helping customers identify their needs, managers have to be careful in moving from one kind of encounter to another. Such transitions from one encounter to another affect crucial organizational properties.

Essentially, structures that would optimize the employee's direct involvement with the client/customer would have to be consistent with an atmosphere in which the preeminent characteristic is self-regulation. In the face of high task uncertainty and where there is little job interdependence, entrepreneurial self-control is thought to lead to more effective use of resources (Slocum and Sims 1980; Mills 1983). This seems to establish broad task boundaries within which the service employee can utilize his or her discretion and knowledge. An important point here is that these kinds of activities increase the power of lower participants in service organizations and serve as a clear demarcation between lower participants in services and their manufacturing counterparts.

Chapters 4 and 5 discussed two kinds of structures: objective and value. These control mechanisms have direct bearing on the organizing framework of service operations. Objective structural constraints (the specificity of position and the description of such position, the extent to which there is reliance on detailed formal rules and procedures, the degree of lower level employees in the decisionmaking process, and so on) will be of only miniscule effect in regulating the behaviors of service providers. This is because after people have held a job for a short time, objective structural constraints become redundant.

What is more important in securing consistency of behavior and is also in keeping with the dictates of self-regulation is the value structure of the organization. Value structures are essential coping mechanisms that enable the service provider to address pertinent areas of uncertainty. Such structures intervene as a referable standard for narrowing choices for the service provider. It is unfortunate that so little attention has been directed at value structures as such structures are potentially viable mechanisms for reducing organizing costs in service operations.

Significant competitive advantages can be realized by the service manager who seriously considers clients/customers as partial employees. This perspective would recognize the operations of services as consumer intensive and that clients and customers are potential sources of production. In order to mobilize the consumer's effort efficiently, service organizations will have to devote resources not only to developing their production roles, but also to establishing more elaborate socialization strategies for client/customer participation.

REFERENCES

Adam, E.; J. Hershauer; and W. Ruch. 1981. *Productivity and Quality: Measurement as a Basis for Improvement.* Englewood Cliffs, N.J.: Prentice Hall.

Adams, J. 1965. "Toward an Understanding of Inequity." *Journal of Abnormal and Social Psychology* 67: 422–436.

Allport, F. 1962. "A Structuronomic Conception of Behavior: Individual and Collective." *Journal of Abnormal and Social Psychology* 64: 3–30.

Ansoff, I., and R. Brandenburg. 1971. "A Language for Organization." *Management Science* 11: 711–731.

Bachrach, S., and E. Lawler. 1980. *Power and Politics in Organizations.* San Francisco: Jossey-Bass.

Barnard, C. 1938. *The Function of the Executive.* Cambridge, Mass.: Harvard University Press.

Bateson, J. 1985. "Perceived Control and the Service Encounter." In *The Service Encounter,* edited by John Czepiel, Michael Solomon, and Carol Surprenant, pp. 67–82. Lexington, Mass.: Lexington Books.

Bauer, R. 1968. "Consumer Behavior as Risk Taking." In *Marketing and the Behavioral Sciences: Selected Readings,* edited by P. Bliss, pp. 55–65. Boston: Allyn and Bacon.

Bazerman, M. 1982. "Impact of Personal Control on Performance: Is Added Control Always Beneficial?" *Journal of Applied Psychology* 67: 472–479.

Bell, D. 1973. *The Coming of Post-Industrial Society.* New York: Basic Books.

Bell, G. 1965. "Determinants of Span of Control." *American Journal of Sociology* 73: 100–109.

193

Berry, L. 1984. "Services Marketing Is Different." In *Services Marketing*, edited by Christopher Lovelock, pp. 29–37. Englewood Cliffs, N.J.: Prentice-Hall.

Blalock, H., and A. Blalock. 1968. *Methodology in Social Research*. New York: McGraw-Hill.

Blau, P.M., and W.R. Scott. 1962. *Formal Organizations: A Comparative Approach*. San Francisco: Chandler Publishing.

Bobbitt, R., and J. Ford. 1980. "Decision Maker Choice as a Determinate of Organizational Structure." *Academy of Management Review* 5: 13–23.

Bowen, D., and B. Schneider. 1985. "Boundary-Spanning-Role Employee and the Service Encounter: Some Guidelines for Management and Research." In *The Service Encounter*, edited by John Czepiel, Michael Solomon, and Carol Surprenant, pp. 127–147. Lexington, Mass.: Lexington Books.

Brim, O. 1966. "Socialization through the Life Cycle." In *Socialization after Childhood: Two Essays*, edited by O. Brim and S. Wheeler, pp. 1–49. New York: Wiley.

Brown, M. 1976. "Values—A Necessary but Neglected Ingredient of Motivation on the Job." *Academy of Management Review* 1: 15–23.

Browning, C., and J. Singlemann. 1978. "The Transformation of the U.S. Labor Force: The Interaction of Industry and Occupation." *Politics and Society* 8: 451–509.

Bucher, R., and J. Stelling. 1969. "Characteristics of Professional Organizations." *Journal of Health and Social Behavior* 10: 3–15.

Cameron, K. 1981. "Construct Space and Subjectivity Problems in Organizational Effectiveness." *Public Productivity Review* (June): 105–121.

Chase, R. 1978. "Where Does the Customer Fit in a Service Operation?" *Harvard Business Review* 56, no. 6: 137–142.

Chase, R., and D. Tansik. 1982. "The Customer Contact Model for Organization Design." *Management Science* 29: 1037–1050.

Child, J., and R. Mansfield. 1974. "Technology, Size, and Organization Structure." *Sociology* 6: 369–393.

Clark, C. 1957. *The Conditions of Economic Progress*. 3d ed. London: Mac-Millan.

Clegg, S. 1981. "Organization and Control." *Administrative Science Quarterly* 26: 120–128.

Cleland, D. 1969. "Understanding Project Authority." *Business Horizons* 10: 63–76.

Coase, R. 1952. "The Nature of the Firm." In *Readings in Price Theory*, edited by G. Stigler and K. Boulding, pp. 331–351. Homewood, Ill.: Irwin.

Corwin, R. 1969. "Patterns of Organizational Conflict." *Administrative Science Quarterly* 26: 545–562.

Cyert, R., and J. March. 1963. *A Behavioral Theory of the Firm*. Englewood Cliffs, N.J.: Prentice-Hall.

Daft, R. 1978. "A Dual Core of Organizational Innovation." *Academy of Management Journal* 21, 193–210.

Daft, R., and N. Macintosh. 1981. "A Tentative Exploration into the Amount and Equivocality of Information Processing in Organizational Work Units." *Administrative Science Quarterly* 26: 207–234.

_____. 1984. "The Nature and Use of Formal Control Systems for Management Control and Strategy Implementation." *Journal of Management* 10, 43–66.

Davis, L., and J. Taylor, eds. 1972. *Design of Jobs.* Middlesex, England: Penguin Books.

Davis, S. 1983. "Management Models for the Future." *New Management* 1: 12–15.

Delbecq, A., and P. Mills. 1985. "Managerial Practices that Enhance Innovation." *Organization Dynamics*, Summer, 24–34.

Dewar, R.; D. Whetten; and D. Boje. 1980. "An Examination of the Reliability and Validity of the Aiken and Hage Scales of Centralization, Formalization and Task Routines." *Administrative Science Quarterly* 26: 120–128.

Doeringer, P., and M. Piore. 1971. *Internal Labor Markets and Manpower Analysis.* Lexington, Mass.: Lexington Books.

Dubin, R. 1956. "Industrial Workers' World: A Study of the Central Life Interests of Industrial Workers." *Social Problems* 3: 131–142.

_____. 1958. *The World of Work.* Englewood Cliffs, N.J.: Prentice-Hall.

_____. 1959. "Stability of Human Organizations." In *Modern Organization Theory*, edited by M. Haire, pp. 218–253. New York: Wiley.

_____. 1963. "Power Functions and Organizations." *Pacific Sociological Reviews* 6: 16–24.

_____. 1968. *Human Relations in Administration.* 3d ed. Englewood Cliffs, N.J.: Prentice-Hall.

Dubin, R.; J. Champaux; and L. Porter. 1975. "Central Life Interests and Organizational Commitment of Blue Collar and Clerical Workers." *Administrative Science Quarterly* 20: 411–421.

Dubin, R.; G. Homans; F. Mann; and D. Miller. 1965. *Leadership and Productivity.* San Francisco: Chandler Publishing Company.

Duncan, R.B. 1972. "Characteristics of Organizational Environments and Perceived Environmental Uncertainty." *Administrative Science Quarterly* 17: 313–327.

Dunnette, M. 1966. *Personnel Selection and Placement.* Belmont, Calif.: Wadsworth.

Durkheim, E. 1933. *The Division of Labor in Society.* New York: The MacMillan Company.

Emery, E.F., and E.L. Trist. 1965. "The Causal Texture of Organizational Environment." *Human Relations* 18: 21–32.

Evans, P. 1975. "Multiple Hierarchies and Organization Control." *Administrative Science Quarterly* 20: 250–271.

Fama, E. 1980. "Agency Problems and the Theory of the Firm." *Journal of Political Economics* 88: 258-307.

Fama, E., and M. Jensen. 1983. "Agency Problems and Residual Claims." *Journal of Law and Economics* 26: 327-349.

Feldman, D. 1981. "The Multiple Socialization of Organization Members." *Academy of Management Review* 6: 309-318.

Fitzsimons, J., and R. Sullivan. 1982. *Service Operations Management.* New York: McGraw-Hill.

Fox, R. 1959. *Experiment Perilous.* New York: Free Press.

Friedson, E. 1970. *The Profession of Medicine.* New York: Dodd, Mead.

_____. 1973. "Professionalism and the Organization of Labor in Post-Industrial Society." *The Sociological Review Monograph* 20: 47-59.

Fuchs, V. 1968. *The Service Economy.* National Bureau of Economic Research. New York: Columbia University Press.

Galbraith, J. 1973. *Designing Complex Organizations.* Reading, Mass.: Addison-Wesley.

Galbraith, J.K. 1969. *The Affluent Society.* 2d ed. London: Hamish Hamilton.

Gartner, A., and F. Reissman. 1974. *The Service Society and the Consumer Vanguard.* New York: Harper & Row.

_____. 1977. *Self-Help in the Human Services.* San Francisco: Jossey-Bass.

Gellerman, S. 1968. *Management by Motivation.* New York: American Management Association, Inc.

George, W.; M. Weinberger; and P. Kelly. 1985. "Consumer Rick Perceptions: Managerial Tool for the Service Encounter." In *The Service Encounter,* edited by John Czepiel, Michael Colomon, and Carol Surprenant, pp. 83-100. Lexington, Mass.: Lexington Books.

Gershuny, J., and I. Miles. 1983. *The Service Economy.* London: Frances Pinter.

Glisson, C. 1978. "Dependence of Technology Routinization on Structural Variables in Human Service Organizations." *Administrative Science Quarterly* 28: 384-395.

Goffman, E. 1983. "The Interaction Order." *American Sociological Review* 48: 1-17.

Graen, G. 1976. "Role-Making Processes within Complex Organizations." In *Handbook of Industrial and Organizational Psychology,* edited by M. Dunnette, pp. 1201-1245. New York: Rand-McNally.

Grossman, M., and V. Fuchs. 1973. "Intersectional Shifts and Aggregate Productivity Change." *Annals of Economic and Social Measurement* 2: 227-243.

Hackman, R.; G. Oldham; R. Janson; and K. Purdy. 1975. "A New Strategy for Job Enrichment." *California Management Review,* Summer, 57-71.

Hage, J., and M. Aiken. 1969. "Routine Technology, Social Structure and Organizational Goals." *Administrative Science Quarterly* 14: 366-376.

Hall, R. 1968. "Professionalization and Bureaucratization." *American Sociological Review* 33: 92-104.

Heilbroner, R. 1980. *The Making of Economic Society.* 6 ed. Englewood Cliffs, N.J.: Prentice-Hall.

Hernes, G. 1975. *Power and Collective Decisions: Extensions Applications.* Memorandum No. 38. Bergen, Norway: Maktotredningen, Bergen University.

Hogan, J.; R. Hogan; and C. Busch. 1984. "How To Measure Service Orientation." *Journal of Applied Psychology* 69: 167–173.

Holstrom, B. 1982. "The Provision of Services in a Market Economy." Paper presented at the ARA/Wharton Conference, The Wharton School, University of Pennsylvania, November 19–20.

Homans, G. 1950. *The Human Group.* New York: Harcourt Brace.

Hrebiniak, I. 1974. "Job Technology, Supervision and Work Group Structure." *Administrative Science Quarterly* 19: 394–410.

Hunt R. 1970. "Technology and Organization." *Academy of Management Journal* 13: 235–252.

James, L., and A. Jones. 1976. "Organization Structure: A Review of Structural Dimensions and Their Conceptual Relationships with Individual Attitudes and Behavior." *Organizational Behavior and Human Performance* 16: 74–113.

Jensen, M., and W. Meckling. 1976. "Theory of the Firm: Managerial Behavior, Agency Costs and Ownership Structure." *Journal of Financial Economics* 3: 305–360.

Jobson, J., and R. Schneck. 1982. Constituent Views of Organizational Effectiveness: Evidence from Police Organizations." *Academy of Management Journal* 25: 25–46.

Kaldor, N. 1966. *Causes of Slow Economic Growth of U.K.* London: Cambridge University Press.

Kalleberg, A. 1977. "Work Values and Job Rewards: A Theory of Job Satisfaction." *American Sociological Review* 42: 126–143.

Katz, D. 1964. "The Motivational Basis of Organizational Behavior." *Behavioral Science* 9: 131–164.

Katz, D., and R. Kahn. 1978. "The Social Psychology of Organizations. New York: Wiley.

Kavis, I.; A. Heston; and R. Summers. 1978. "Real GNP Per Capita for More Than One-Hundred Countries." *Economic Journal* 88: 215–241.

Keller, R. 1975. "Role Conflict and Ambiguity: Correlates with Job Satisfaction and Values." *Personnel Psychology* 18: 57–64.

Kelley, H. 1967. "Attribution Theory in Social Psychology." In *Nebraska: Symposium on Motivation,* vol. 15, edited by D. Levine, pp. 192–238. Lincoln: University of Nebraska Press.

Kelly, J. 1969. *Organization Behavior.* Homewood, Ill.: Richard D. Irwin, Inc. and the Dorsey Press.

Kemper, T. 1968. "Reference Groups, Socialization and Achievement." *American Sociological Review* 33: 31–45.

Kerlinger, F., and E. Pedhazur. 1973. *Multiple Regression in Behavioral Research.* New York: Holt, Rinehart & Winston.

Klaus, P. 1985. "Quality Epiphenomenon: The Conceptual Understanding of Quality in Face-to-Face Service Encounters." In *The Service Encounter*, edited by John Czepiel, Michael Solomon, and Carol Surprenant, pp. 17–33. Lexington, Mass.: Lexington Books.

Klein, B. 1983. "Contracting Costs and Residual Claims: The Separation of Ownership and Control." *Journal of Law and Economics* 26: 367–374.

Kluckholn, C. 1952. "Values and Value-Orientation in the Theory of Action." In *Towards a General Theory of Action*, edited by T. Parsons and Edward Shils, pp. 388–433. Cambridge, Mass.: Harvard University Press.

Kolodny, H. 1979. "Evolution to a Matrix Organization." *Academy of Management Review* 4: 547–553.

Korsch, B., and V. Negreta. 1972. "Doctor-Patient Communication." *Scientific America* 228: 66–74.

Langeard, E.; J. Bateson; C. Lovelock; and P. Eiglier. 1981. *Marketing of Services: New Insights from Consumers and Managers.* Report No. 81-104. Cambridge, Mass.: Marketing Science Institute.

Lawrence, P., and J. Lorsch. 1967. *Organization and Environment.* Cambridge, Mass.: Harvard University Press.

Lee, D. 1948. "Are Basic Needs Ultimate?" *Journal of Abnormal and Social Psychology* 43: 391–395.

Leftwich, R. 1966. *The Price System and Resource Allocation.* 3d ed. New York: Holt, Rinehart & Winston.

Leibenstein, H. 1976. *Beyond Economic Man.* Cambridge: Harvard University Press.

Levitt, T. 1972. "Production-Line Approach to Service." *Harvard Business Review* 50, no. 5: 41–52.

Lewin, K. 1936. *A Dynamic Theory of Personality.* New York: McGraw-Hill.

Litterer, J. 1965. *The Analysis of Organizations.* New York: Wiley.

Litwin, G., and R. Stringer. 1968. *Motivation and Organizational Climate.* Cambridge, Mass.: Harvard University Press.

Locke, E. 1969. "What is Job Satisfaction?" *Organization Behavior and Human Performance* 4, 309–36.

Longest, B. 1977. "Productivity in the Provision of Hospital Services: A Challenge to the Management Community." *Academy of Management Review* (July): 475–483.

Louis, M. 1980. "Surprise and Sense Making: What Newcomers Experience in Entering Unfamiliar Organizational Settings. *Administrative Science Quarterly* 25: 226–251.

Maister, D. 1983. *Professional Service Firm Management.* Boston: Harvard Business School.

Mark, J. 1981. "Measuring Productivity in Government." *Public Productivity Review* 5 (March): 21–44.

McCallum, R., and W. Harrison. 1985. "Interdependence in the Service Encounter." In *The Service Encounter*, edited by John Czepiel, Michael Solomon, and Carol Surprenant, pp. 35–48. Lexington, Mass.: Lexington Books.

McDonough, J. 1975. "One Day in the Life of Ivan Denisovich: A Study of the Structural Requisite of Organizations. *Human Relations* 24: 295–338.

McMahon, T., and J. Ivancevich. 1971. "A Study of Control in Manufacturing Organization: Managers and Non-Managers." *Administrative Science Quarterly* 16: 151–163.

McNeal, J. 1964. *Children as Consumers.* Austin: University of Texas, Bureau of Business Research.

Merton, R. 1957. *Social Theory and Social Structure.* Rev. ed. New York: Free Press.

Meyer, J., and B. Rowan. 1977. "Institutionalized Organizations: Formal Structure as Myth and Ceremony." *American Journal of Sociology* 83, 340–363.

Miller, E., and A. Rice. 1967. *Systems of Organizations.* London: Tavistock Publications.

Mills, P. 1983. "Self-Management: Its Control and Relationship to Other Organizational Properties." *Academy of Management Review* 8: 445–453.

Mills, P.; R. Chase; and N. Margulies. 1983. "Motivating the Client/Employee System as a Service Production Strategy." *Academy of Management Review* 8: 301–310.

Mills, P.; J. Hall; J. Leidecker; and N. Margulies. 1983. "Flexiform: A Model for Professional Service Organizations." *Academy of Management Review* 8: 118–131.

Mills, P., and N. Margulies. 1980. "Toward a Core Typology of Service Organizations." *Academy of Management Review* 5: 255–265.

Mills, P., and D. Moberg. 1982. "Perspectives on the Technology of Service Operations." *Academy of Management Review* 7: 467–478.

Mills, P., and B. Posner. 1982. "The Relationship Among Self-Supervision, Structure, and Technology in Professional Service Organizations." *Academy of Management Journal* 25, 437–443.

Mintzberg, H. 1979. *The Structuring of Organizations.* Englewood Cliffs, N.J.: Prentice-Hall.

Mohr, L. 1969. "Determinants of Innovation in Organizations." *American Political Science Review* 63: 111–126.

_____. 1971. "Organizational Technology and Organizational Structure. *Administrative Science Quarterly* 16: 444–459.

Ouchi, W., and M. Maguire. 1975. "Organizational Control: Two Functions." *Administrative Science Quarterly* 20: 559–569.

Parks, R. 1984. "Linking Objective and Subjective Measures of Performance." *Public Administration Review* 8 (March-April): 118–127.

Parsons, T. 1964. "The Monopoly of Force and the Power Bank." In *Internal War*, edited by Harry Eckstein, pp. 57–65. New York: Free Press.

Payne, R., and D. Pugh. 1976. "Organizational Structure and Climate." In *Handbook of Industrial and Organizational Psychology*, edited by M. Dunnette, pp. 1125–1173. Chicago: Rand-McNally.

Perrow, C. 1967. "A Framework for the Comparative Analysis of Organizations." *American Sociological Review* 32: 196–208.

Pfeffer, J. 1978. *The External Control of Organizations: A Resource Dependence Perspective*. New York: Harper & Row.

Pondy, L. 1967. "Organizational Conflict: Concepts and Models." *Administrative Science Quarterly* 12: 296–320.

Popper, K. 1962. *The Open Society and Its Enemies*. 2 vols. Princeton, N.J.: Princeton University Press.

Porter, L., and E. Lawler. 1968. *Managerial Attitudes and Performance*. Homewood, Ill.: Irwin.

Prescott, E., and M. Visscher. 1980. "Organization Capital." *Journal of Political Economy* 88: 446–461.

Pugh, D. S.; D. J. Hickson; C. R. Hinnings; and C. Turner. 1969. "The Context of Organizational Structures." *Administrative Science Quarterly* 13: 229–245.

Reubens, E. 1981. "The Services and Productivity." *Challenge* 24: 59–63.

Roberts, A., and E. Kelly. 1985. "Techniservices and the Organizational Encounter." In *The Service Encounter*, edited by John Czepiel, Michael Solomon, and Carol Surprenant, pp. 283–290. Lexington, Mass.: Lexington Books.

Rohrbaugh, J. 1981. "Operationalizing the Competing Values Approach: Measuring Performance in Employment Service." *Public Productivity Review* 5 (June): 141–159.

Rosengren, W., and M. Lefton, eds. 1970. *Organization and Clients*. Columbus, Ohio: Charles E. Merrill.

Rus, V. 1980. "Positive and Negative Powers: Thoughts on the Dialectics of Power." *Organizational Studies* 1: 3–19.

Sasser, E. 1976. "Match Supply and Demand in Service Industries." *Harvard Business Review* 56, no. 2: 133–148.

Schien, E. 1968. "Organizational Socialization and the Profession of Management." *Industrial Management Review* 9: 1–16.

Schneider, B. 1973. "The Perception of Organizational Climate: The Customer's Views." *Journal of Applied Psychology* 52: 248–256;

Schneider, B., and C. Bartlett. 1970. "Individual Differences and Organizational Climate by the Multi-Trait, Multi-Rater, Matrix." *Personnel Psychology* 23: 493–572.

Schneider, B.; J. Parkington; and V. Buxton. 1980. ,,Employee and Customer Perceptions of Service in Banks." *Administrative Science Quarterly* 25: 252–267.

Scott, W. 1965. *The Management of Conflict: Appeal Systems in Organizations*. Homewood, Ill.: Irwin-Dorsey.

Selznick, P. 1949. *T.V.A. and the Grass Roots.* Berkeley: University of California Press.

Shostack, L. 1977. "Breaking Free from Product Marketing." *Journal of Marketing* 41 (April): 73-80.

Sieber, S. 1974. "Toward a Theory of Role Accumulation." *American Sociological Review* 39: 567-578.

Simmel, G. 1971. *The Problems of the Philosophy of History.* Translated with an introduction by Guy Oakes. New York: Free Press.

Simon, H. 1957. *Administrative Behavior.* 2d ed. New York: MacMillan.

Skår, J. 1971. *Produksjon og produktivitat i detaljhandelen.* Uppsala: Skrive Service AB.

Skogan, W., and M. Maxfield. 1981. *Coping with Crime.* Beverly Hills, Calif.: Sage Publications.

Slocum, J., and H. Simms. 1980. "A Typology for Integrating Technology, Organization and Job Design." *Human Relations* 33: 193-212.

Smith, A. 1904. *The Wealth of Nations.* New York: Dutton & Co.

Solomon, M.; C. Surprenant; J. Czepiel; and G. Gutman. 1985. "A Role Theory Perspective on Dyadic Interactions: The Service Encounter." *Journal of Marketing* 49 (Winter): 99-111.

Stanback, T.; P. Bearse; T. Noyelle; and R. Kapasek. 1981. *Services: The New Economy.* Totowa, N.J.: Allanheld, Osmun & Co.

Stipak, B. 1979. "Citizen Satisfaction with Urban Services: Potential Misuse as a Performance Indicator." *Public Administration Review* 39 (January/February): 46-52.

Stymne, B. 1970. *Values and Processes: A System Study of Effectiveness in the Organization.* Lund, Sweden: Student Literature.

Taylor, F. 1911. *The Principles of Scientific Management.* New York: Harper & Row.

Terrebery, S. 1968. "The Evolution of Organizational Environments." *Administrative Science Quarterly* 12: 590-613.

Thompson, J.D. 1962. "Organizations and Output Transactions." *American Journal of Sociology* 68: 309-324.

_____. 1967. *Organizations in Action.* New York: McGraw-Hill.

Thompson, J., and W. McEwan. 1958. "Organizational Goals and Environment: Goal Setting as an Interactive Process." *American Sociological Review* 23: 23-26.

Van Maanen, J. 1975. "Police Socialization: A Longitudinal Examination of Job Attitudes in an Urban Police Department." *Administrative Science Quarterly* 20: 207-228.

Veblen, T. 1904. *The Theory of the Business Enterprise.* New York: Charles Scribner's Sons.

_____. 1936. "The Cultural Incidence of the Machine." In *What Veblen Taught,* edited by Wesley Mitchell, pp. 302-367. New York: Viking.

Vroom, V. 1964. *Work and Motivation.* New York: Wiley.

Wanous, J. 1973. "Effects of a Realistic Job Preview on Job Acceptance, Job Attitudes and Job Survival." *Journal of Applied Psychology* 58: 327-332.

Ward, S., and D. Wackman. 1973. "Family and Media Influences on Adolescent Consumer Learning." *American Behavioral Scientist* 14: 415-427.

Ward, T. 1973. *The Distribution of Consumer Goods.* Cambridge, Mass.: Harvard University Press.

Warwick, D. 1975. *A Theory of Public Bureaucracy.* Cambridge, Mass.: Harvard University Press.

Weber, M. 1978. *Economy and Society.* Berkeley: University of California Press.

Weick, K. 1969. *The Social Psychology of Organizing.* Reading, Mass.: Addison-Wesley.

_____. 1976. "Educational Organizations as Loosely Coupled Systems." *Administrative Science Quarterly* 21: 1-19.

Willers, D. 1967. "Max Weber's Missing Authority Type." *Sociological Inquiry* 37: 231-239.

Williamson, O. 1975. *Markets and Hierarchies: Analysis and Antitrust Implications.* New York: Free Press.

Woodward, J. 1965. *Industrial Organization: Theory and Practice.* London: Oxford University Press.

Zwerman, W.L. 1970. *New Perspectives on Organization Theory.* Westport, Conn.: Greenwood Publishing.

INDEX

ABOUT THE AUTHOR

Peter K. Mills is an Associate Professor of Management at the University of Santa Clara, California. He holds Ph.D. degrees from both the University of Stockholm, Sweden, and the University of California at Irvine. His research interests lie in the structuring of service organizations, the pricing of performance in service operations, and the economics of power in organizations. Dr. Mills has written for such journals as the *Academy of Management Journal*, the *Academy of Management Review*, the *Journal of Management*, and *Organization Dynamics*.